The Peak Distr

The Peak District

Text by
Robin Whiteman

Photographs by
Rob Talbot

PHOENIX ILLUSTRATED

Text and photographs © Talbot-Whiteman 1997

The right of Robin Whiteman and Rob Talbot to be identified as
authors of this work has been asserted by them in accordance
with the Copyright, Designs and Patents Act 1988.

First published in Great Britain in 1997 by
George Weidenfeld & Nicolson Ltd
The Orion Publishing Group
Orion House
5, Upper St Martin's Lane
London WC2H 9EA

A CIP catalogue record for this book is available
from the British Library.

Designed by Leigh Jones.
Map by Jenny Dooge.
Printed and bound in Italy.

Half-title page: Manifold Valley, from Thor's Cliff.
Frontispiece: Medieval Bridge, Bakewell.

Contents

ACKNOWLEDGEMENTS

Robin Whiteman and Rob Talbot would particularly like to acknowledge the generous co-operation of English Heritage (Historic Properties Midlands & East Anglia) and the two National Trust Regional Offices of Mercia and East Midlands for allowing them to take photographs of their sites featured in this book. Additional thanks go Diana Lanham, Manager of the National Trust Photographic Library. They are also extremely grateful to: The Trustees of the Chatsworth Settlement; and Riber Castle Wildlife Park. The photograph of Haddon Hall was reproduced by permission of Haddon Hall, Bakewell. Appreciation also extends to all those individuals and organizations too numerous to mention by name who nevertheless have made such a valuable contribution.

Other books by Rob Talbot and Robin Whiteman
The Cotswolds
The English Lakes
Shakespeare's Avon
Cadfael Country
The Yorkshire Moors & Dales
The Heart of England
The West Country
Wessex
The Garden of England
English Landscapes
East Anglia & The Fens
Brother Cadfael's Herb Garden

Photographs by Rob Talbot
Shakespeare Country
The Lakeland Poets
Cotswold Villages

Text by Robin Whiteman
The Cadfael Companion

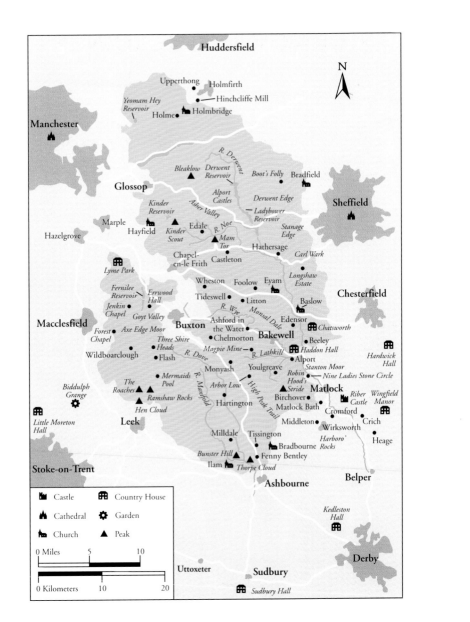

Huddersfield

N

Upperthong
Holmfirth
Hinchcliffe Mill
Yeomam Hey Reservoir
Holme
Holmbridge

Manchester

R. Derwent

Bleaklow
Derwent Reservoir
Boot's Folly
Bradfield

Glossop

Alport Castles
Derwent Edge

Kinder Reservoir
Ashop Valley
Ladybower Reservoir

Sheffield

Marple
R. Noe
Stanage Edge

Hazelgrove
Hayfield
Kinder Scout
Edale
Mam Tor
Hathersage
Carl Wark

Chapel-en-le-Frith
Castleton

Lyme Park
Wheston
Foolow
Eyam
Longshaw Estate

Fernilee Reservoir
Errwood Hall
Tideswell
Litton
Baslow

Jenkin Chapel
Goyt Valley

Chesterfield

Macclesfield
Axe Edge Moor
Buxton
Ashford in the Water
Monsal Dale
Edensor
Chatsworth

Forest Chapel
Three Shire Heads
Chelmorton
Bakewell
Beeley

Wildboarclough
Flash
R. Dove
Magpie Mine
R. Lathkill
Haddon Hall
Alport
Hardwick Hall

Mermaids Pool
Monyash
Youlgreave
Stanton Moor
Nine Ladies Stone Circle

Biddulph Grange
The Roaches
Arbor Low
R. Manifold
Robin Hood's Stride
Matlock

Ramshaw Rocks
Hartington
High Peak Trail
Birchover
Riber Castle
Wingfield Manor

Hen Cloud
Matlock Bath
Cromford

Leek
Milldale
Tissington
Middleton
Wirksworth
Crich
Heage

Little Moreton Hall
Bunster Hill
Bradbourne
Harboro' Rocks

Ilam
Thorpe Cloud
Fenny Bentley

Stoke-on-Trent
Belper

Ashbourne

Castle
Country House

Cathedral
Garden

Church
Peak

0 Miles   5   10

0 Kilometers   10   20

Uttoxeter
Sudbury
Derby

Kedleston Hall

Sudbury Hall

STANAGE EDGE
near Hathersage

The history of rock-climbing in the Peak District dates from 1885 when J.W. Puttrell, at the age of sixteen, ascended the Prow Rock on Wharncliffe Crags, near Stocksbridge. Five years later, he also became the first to climb the crags at Stanage Edge – the long, broken wall of precipitous gritstone, which runs north from the Cowper Stone for some 4 miles, and is now one of the most popular climbing sites in England. 'This region', wrote Walt Unsworth in *The English Outcrops* (1964), 'is the Valhalla of the gritstoner, and within it the Throne of the Gods is Stanage Edge.' The highest point of the 'edge', High Neb, reaches 1,502 feet above sea level. An opening in the rocks, known as Robin Hood's Cave, is one of several natural features in the area associated with the outlaw. Sited at regular intervals along the 'edge' are a series of small, numbered drinking basins. They were cut in the gritstone by gamekeepers at the beginning of the twentieth century to ensure that their grouse had a ready supply of acid-free water.

INTRODUCTION

William Camden, in his classic work *Britannia* (first published in 1586), mentioned 'nine things that please us at the Peak', yet only three – 'a Cave, a Den, and Hole' – were described as 'wonders'. It seems that the first to specify 'Seven Wonders of the Peak' was the Warwickshire poet, Michael Drayton. In the second part of his topographical poem on England, *Poly-Olbion*, completed in 1622, he included an allegorical map of Derbyshire, Nottinghamshire and Leicestershire followed by a poem – 'The Sixe and Twentieth Song' – relating to the three counties. In the order of Drayton's 'unfolding', the Peak's seven wonders were: 'The Divels-Arse' (Peak Cavern, Castleton); 'Pooles Hole' (Poole's Cavern, Buxton); 'Elden Hole' (Eldon Hole, near the village of Peak Forest); 'Saint Anne of Buckston' (St Ann's Well, Buxton); 'Tydeswell' (the Ebbing-and-Flowing Well, Tideswell); 'Sandy Hill' (Mam Tor, Castleton); and 'The Peake Forrest' (The Royal Forest of the Peak).

In 1636, fourteen years after the publication of Drayton's twenty-sixth song, Thomas Hobbes mentioned seven wonders in his Latin poem *De Mirabilibus Pecci* (*Concerning the Wonders of the Peak*). With one significant exception, they were almost identical to Drayton's. Hobbes' one-line summary of the wonders – 'house, mountain, pit, two fountains, and two caves' – referred, respectively, to Chatsworth House, Mam Tor, Eldon Hole, St Ann's Well, the ebbing-and-flowing well in Barmoor Clough (near Sparrowpit), Poole's Cavern, and Peak Cavern. Indeed, as the owners of Chatsworth, the Cavendish family, were Hobbes' patrons, it is not surprising that their house should head his list of wonders. Charles Cotton, squire of Beresford Hall, not only rehashed Hobbes' list in *The Wonders of the Peak* (1681), he also dedicated the poem to the 'Right Honourable Elizabeth Countess of Devonshire' (wife of the 3rd Earl, William Cavendish).

For many early travellers to the Peak District, like Celia Fiennes and Daniel Defoe, viewing the wonders became an essential part of their itinerary. Fiennes travelled through Derbyshire in 1697 and, in her manuscript journal (first published in an incomplete version in 1888 under the title *Through England on a Side Saddle in the Time of William and Mary*), she described each wonder in turn, starting with Chatsworth House (the rebuilding of which had almost been completed) and ending with the 'Flowing and Ebbing Well' at Tideswell. Defoe visited the region in 1712 and, in *A Tour Thro' the Whole Island of Great Britain* (1724–26), he dismissed most of the wonders as 'trifles'. After being far from impressed by five of the 'wonderless wonders of the Peak', Defoe concluded: 'so much for fictitious wonders, or indeed simple wonders'. The two real wonders which remain, are first, Eldon Hole, and second, the Duke of Devonshire's fine house at Chatsworth; one a wonder of nature, the other of art.

Having read Cotton's *The Wonders of the Peak* (about which which he had 'always wondered more at the poetry than at the Peak'), Defoe felt obliged to see the River Dove, 'which that Gentleman has spent so much doggerel upon, and celebrated to such a degree for trout and grayling'. By way of contrast to Defoe's lukewarm reaction, later literary figures, like Dr Johnson (1709–84) and Lord Byron (1788–1824), favourably compared the scenery of Dovedale to that found in more mountainous regions of Britain and Europe. The romantic view of 'picturesque' scenery was echoed in the watercolours of Dovedale by Joseph Wright of Derby (1734–97) and in the Derbyshire oil paintings of George Turner (1843–1910). The scenery enjoyed by the Victorians was so influential in Dovedale that the National Trust, who own most of the dale, have made a conscious decision to maintain the landscape in accordance with the romantic vision of 150 years ago. Today, Dovedale – with its dramatic rock features, water-worn caves, steep scree slopes, ancient woodland and dipper-frequented stream – is one of the most popular tourist destinations in the Peak District.

The limestone of the so-called White Peak, within which Dovedale is situated, was formed some 350 million years ago, in the Carboniferous period, when the landscape was very different – namely, blue lagoons, fringed by coral reefs, washed by the clear waters of a shallow tropical sea. In essence, the rock is composed of the fossilized remains of primitive sea organisms, their shells accumulating as sediment, either on the lagoon bottom to create bedded layers, or combining with the coral to form unbedded reef limestones. Despite the fact that limestone is a rock of great hardness and durability (hence its reputation for being an excellent building material), its inherent weakness is that it is very porous and can be dissolved by slightly acid rainwater. As the water percolates downwards through vertical joints and bedding planes, so hairline cracks are gradually widened over time to create an intricate network of underground passages, potholes and cave systems. Sand, stones and other debris carried by running water also helped to enlarge the expanding channels. Curiously, in the Manifold Valley the limestone river bed is often dry because the main body of water suddenly disappears down a 'swallet hole' at one point, only to re-emerge 6 miles away in a 'boil hole' at another. In Dovedale the harder reef limestones, which are more resilient to erosion, are not only responsible for creating the winding course of the river, they also form pinnacles, such as Ilam Rock. A few of the gorges elsewhere in the Peak, if only in part, were created by the collapse of underground cave systems. Stalactites and other formations, like the delicate straws and iron-stained 'poached eggs' found in Poole's Cavern, Buxton, have been built up over thousands of years by water dripping from the roof of a cave. After percolating through the limestone, the water leaves tiny deposits of calcite which accumulate to form a breathtaking variety of pillars and column-shaped rocks.

Gritstone or Millstone Grit, the other predominant rock in the Peak District, was formed of river-borne sands and gravels, which were deposited at deltas on top of the Carboniferous limestone. Unlike the limestone, however, the rock is much more impervious to water and, therefore, the gritstone landscape is characterized by vast areas of badly drained peat moorlands, broken up by drainage channels known as 'groughs'. In places, the harder blocks of gritstone (known as 'tors') – left behind after the erosion of softer sandstones – have been sculpted by wind, frost and rain into an extraordinary assortment of shapes. Incidentally, the softer shales and sandstones (which sandwiched together with the coarser Millstone Grit may reach a thickness of over 2,000 feet) were formed from the accumulation of sands and muds. The alternating layers of sedimentary material can be clearly seen on the exposed east face of Mam Tor. Its colourful name, the 'Shivering Mountain', comes from the unstable nature of the layers, which easily crumble to cause landslips. One final series of rocks worth mentioning, also laid down during the Carboniferous period, are the Coal Measures, formed from the luxurious vegetation and waterlogged wood of tropical forest swamps. In the Peak District most of the Coal Measures have been eroded away, leaving only the occasional outcropping seam, notably in the Goyt Valley and near the Roaches.

After the various sedimentary rocks of the Carboniferous period had been formed, cataclysmic movements in the earth's crust lifted up the area that was to be the southern Pennines to create a massive dome, parts of which were crumpled into a series of folds. Over time, the all-powerful forces of erosion wore away the Coal Measures, shales and millstone grit in the centre of the Peak to expose the limestones beneath. The evidence of further changes in the climate, which brought desert as well as the return of the sea, has been almost entirely wiped away in the Peak District by erosion. After millions of years in the making, the last great transformation of the Peakland landscape (which, in effect, refined the details) occurred during the Ice Ages, when the crushing and abrasive power of glacial advances and retreats, together with huge volumes of meltwater, created many of the natural features so distinctive to the region.

With reference to the scenery today, the Peak District embraces the most southerly part of the Pennines, thereby marking the transition from lowland to highland England. Its two strongly contrasting landscapes, known as the Dark Peak and the White Peak, each with its own distinct character, are based on the predominant rock: the former being gritstone and the latter limestone. The Dark Peak, north of Castleton, is also known as the High Peak and embraces the wildest country, the remotest farms and the highest hills. Furthermore, the gritstone extends south for several miles down both the eastern and western sides of the region to create a horseshoe around the central White Peak. These perpendicular gritstone 'edges' are not only impressive as landscape features, they have also become a mecca for rock-climbers.

The campaign for public access to the privately-owned grouse moors of the Dark Peak was brought to national attention by the arrest and imprisonment of five ramblers who took part in the historic 'mass trespass' on Kinder Scout in 1932. Seventeen years later, Parliament passed the National Parks and Access to the Countryside Act and, after the creation of the Peak National Park in 1951, agreements were reached with landowners to open large areas of the northern moors to the public (except during the days of grouse shooting).

For the purpose of this book, the Peak District embraces a slightly larger area than the 555 square miles of the National Park. Inevitably, in such a popular and uniquely varied region (rich in customs and folklore as well as history, architecture and landscape), the potential for listing far more wonders than the traditional seven is enormous. Yet, of this there can be little doubt, the *real* wonder of wonders has to be the Peak National Park itself – the first to be so-designated in the whole of England and Wales. 'Not ours,' as Brian Redhead said after becoming President for the Council for National Parks in 1986, 'but ours to look after.'

THE ROACHES AND HEN CLOUD

Rising to over 1,500 feet above sea level, the dark, buttressed ridge of the Roaches forms one of the most impressive gritstone outcrops in the whole of the Peak District. Not surprisingly, rock-climbers are drawn to its formidable crags like a powerful magnet. The name 'Roaches' is thought to derive from the French for 'rocks'. Covering almost 1,000 acres, the Roaches Estate was purchased by the Peak National Park in 1979, and supports an amazing variety of wildlife, including a small colony of red-necked wallabies, the latter being descendants of animals that escaped from a private collection at nearby Swythamley Park in the 1940s. Hen Cloud, the isolated southern extension of the Roaches, rises steeply from the moor to 1,240 feet. Lud's Church, in the depths of the Back Forest near Gradbach, a mile or so north-west of the Roaches, is a deep gritstone chasm created by a huge landslip. Tradition says that it is the legendary Green Chapel mentioned in the medieval alliterative poem *Sir Gawain and the Green Knight*.

Ashbourne and the Southern Peak

The medieval church of the Holy Cross at Ilam was largely restored in the 1850s. The octagonal mausoleum on the north side was added some thirty years earlier by Jesse Watts-Russell to commemorate his father-in-law, David Pyke-Watts. Fragments of the Anglo-Saxon church which originally stood on the site can be found in the blocked doorway of the south wall. In the churchyard are the shafts of two tenth-century crosses. The Anglo-Saxon font, carved with figures and beasts, is said to depict scenes from the life of St Bertram (sometimes spelt 'Bertelin' or 'Bettelin'), whose tomb partly survives inside the Chapel of St Bertram (built in 1618). Tradition says that he was the son of a Mercian king, who renounced his royal heritage to become a hermit after his wife and new-born child were killed by wolves. During the Middle Ages his shrine at Ilam was a place of pilgrimage, and the scene of many miraculous cures. The upper part of the church tower, including the saddleback roof, dates from the Victorian restoration.

Each year, after being given lunch at the Green Man Hotel, Ashbourne, a local or national personality is handed a brightly painted, cork-stuffed football and invited to throw it into the air above the heads of the waiting crowd. Their action marks the start of up to eight hours of shove-and-scramble through the streets of the old market town. Although entitled Royal Shrovetide Football, the game bears few similarities to the sport: there are almost no rules; the ball can be handled as well as kicked; hundreds of players may be involved; and the goals are some three miles apart (one at Sturston and the other at Clifton). As these two objectives are on the southern banks of the Henmore Brook, much of the action inevitably takes place in the water. Those players that live on the north side of the river belong to the Up'ards team, and those on the south the Down'ards. The game ends when a player bangs the ball three times against his or her own goal. The only woman to have ever scored was a Mrs Muggleston. More often than not, however, the game is ended without either team achieving victory. Attempts to ban the game, especially in the late nineteenth century, came to nothing. On one occasion the ball was smuggled through the police cordon in the basket of a fruit seller, then thrown out of the window of an attorney's house into the crowded Market Place. The game's 'royal' title dates from Shrove Tuesday 1928, when the Prince of Wales (later King Edward VIII) 'turned up' the ball to start the game.

Royal Shrovetide Football may be unique to Ashbourne, but many other ancient and traditional customs have been retained throughout the Peak District, the most widespread being well-dressing. Although its origins may lie in pre-Christian times, well-dressing in its present form is said to date back to the mid-fourteenth century, when the Black Death ravaged England. According to tradition, the inhabitants of Tissington escaped contamination by drinking the pure water that issued from the village's wells. By way of thanksgiving, the wells were dressed with flowers. Today the annual blessing of the wells involves the creation of elaborate floral pictures, usually based on a religious theme. In *The Beauty and Mystery of Well-Dressing* (1949) Crichton Porteous wrote:

One of the most difficult tasks is the gathering of all the colours wanted, and in some years the country round may have to be searched for miles. The more methodical dressers have all their materials pulled to bits and sorted beforehand, so that one may watch them surrounded by little mounds and pools of petals, bracts, buds and so on, each mound and pool of a different shade from which they select as a painter selects among the mixtures on his palette.

Although there have been long breaks in the annual continuity of the custom at Tissington, the village is generally considered to be the 'mother-place of well-dressing', with thousands of people attending the week-long event, starting on Ascension Day.

Well-dressing is mainly restricted to the limestone villages of the White Peak, where streams have a habit of drying up or disappearing underground, thereby making the gift of a never-failing spring or well something to cherish and give thanks for. Other lapsed customs to do with water, include 'Sugar Cupping' at Tideswell and Ashford-in-the-Water, dropping new pins into the wells at Bradwell, and 'Bottle Day' at Chapel-en-le-Frith. Most of these practices curiously involved adding water to liquorice. For example, in the nineteenth century at Chapel-en-le-Frith every child was given a bottle containing sugar and liquorice, which, after filling with water, they proceeded to shake and suck for the rest of the day. Chapel-en-le-Frith, among other places, was also the scene of an annual rush-bearing ceremony, commemorating the renewal of rushes on church floors. Today, however, the only place in the Peak District to retain the ceremony is the remote Forest Chapel, near Macclesfield.

Many of the region's religious customs derive from pagan rituals, which, instead of being suppressed, were absorbed and adapted by the early Christian church. One such ceremony is 'Church Clypping', held at Wirksworth in September, and Burbage, near Buxton, in late July. Today 'clypping' symbolizes the parishioners' love of their church, and involves them joining hands and walking around the outside of the building in a clockwise direction. The 'Woodlands Lovefeast', held annually in a remote barn at Alport Castles Farm, west of Derwent Reservoir, stems from the late seventeenth century when non-conformists were banned by law from assembling to worship God according to the dictates of their own consciences. Today, those who worship at the barn are Methodists. On 12 July 1588 two Roman Catholic priests, who refused to renounce their beliefs and secretly preached in Padley Chapel, near Grindleford Station, were arrested and brought to trial at Derby. Found guilty, they were hung, drawn and quartered. Although the Hall belonging to the Roman Catholic FitzHerbert family is now a ruin, the restored chapel is the focus of an annual pilgrimage, held on the Sunday closest to the day the martyred priests were captured. In Cucklett Delf, Eyam, an annual open-air service is held on the last Sunday in August to honour the villagers who died during the plague of 1665-66.

Morris dancing, which in the Peak District traditionally entails a processional dance, is performed in various villages throughout the region. However, only three within the Peak National Park have their own dance teams – Winster, Tideswell and Castleton. At Castleton, incidentally, the Morris Dance is an integral part of the Garland Ceremony, held each year on Oak-Apple Day (29 May), except when it falls on a Sunday. Both Winster and Tideswell celebrate the traditional annual holiday known as Wakes Week, held around the patronal feast of their respective parish church.

Lead-mining, one of the major Peakland industries, developed its own special laws, customs and privileges, many of which were preserved by Edward Manlove, Steward of the Wirksworth Barmote Court, in the 'Rhymed Chronicle': *The Liberties and Customes of the Lead-Mines Within the Wapentake of Wirksworth* (1653). Lead-mining disputes and claims were officially settled in the Barmote Court, presided over by a barmaster and a jury of miners, with two principal courts at Wirksworth and Monyash: the former dealing with the mines of the Low Peak and the latter those of the High Peak. Punishment for being found guilty of stealing lead for a third time was severe. The offender's hand was impaled up the haft in the stowes (the wooden windlass over a shaft for raising ore), after which he was given an agonizing choice: tear his hand free, or remain and die. The only Barmote Court to survive sits in the Moot Hall at Wirksworth, twice a year, in April and October.

Evidently, despite the disappearance of many Peakland customs – like making funeral garlands for young women who die unmarried, 'Riding the Stang' (carried out when a couple fight or row), and selling the wife – many others have been zealously preserved. Not as fading relics of a distant time, half-remembered, but as a living force, serving to bind the community together in a shared sense of continuity with each other, the earth and the past. Little wonder that annual events like Castleton's 'Garland Day', Tissington's well-dressing, and Ashbourne's 'Royal Shrovetide Football' attract such large and enthusiastic crowds.

PARISH CHURCH
Ashbourne

At the western end of the old market town of Ashbourne stands the parish church of St Oswald, with its spire reaching a height of 212 feet. Occupying the site of an Anglo-Saxon and Norman foundation, the oldest part of the present building above ground is the thirteenth-century chancel. Among the monuments inside the church are memorials to the Cockaynes, the Boothbys and the Bradbournes, all families of local importance. The most celebrated monument is Thomas Banks' white marble effigy of Penelope Boothby, who died in 1791, a month short of her sixth birthday. The inscription reads: 'She was in form and intellect most exquisite. The unfortunate parents ventured their all on this frail bark, and the wreck was total.' Penelope is noted for having had her portrait painted, wearing mob-cap and mittens, by Sir Joshua Reynolds (1723-92). The main churchyard gates, gruesomely embellished with skulls, date from c.1700, but were moved when the road was widened in 1958.

TISSINGTON

Many houses in Tissington – with its green, pond and six wells – bear dates between 1830 and 1861 when the owners of the estate, the FitzHerberts, carried out a major rebuilding programme. The family's original manor house stood near the church. Their present home, Tissington Hall, dates from Jacobean times. It was partly remodelled during the eighteenth century, and in 1902 the Library and Billiard Room wing was completed. Monuments commemorating the FitzHerberts can be found inside the parish church of St Mary, with its squat and unbuttressed Norman tower. Although basically Norman, the building was considerably altered and enlarged during the eighteenth and nineteenth centuries. The finely-turned altar rails are thought to date from 1570-80. Pevsner considered the Norman font, incised with curious beasts, to be 'very barbaric'. It is generally accepted that Tissington is the 'mother-place of well-dressing', with claims that the custom has been going on here since 'time immemorial'.

PARISH CHURCH
Fenny Bentley

Inside the church of St Edmund, King and Martyr, at Fenny Bentley – some 2 miles north of Ashbourne – is the elaborate alabaster tomb-chest of Thomas Beresford and his wife Agnes (née Hassall), who died in 1473 and 1467 respectively. Both effigies are curiously depicted, entirely wrapped up and tied in shrouds. It is thought that this is because they died long before the tomb was erected, and no likenesses were therefore available. Round the sides of the chest are their twenty-one children, all of which are also shrouded. The only child to be named in the inscriptions is their third son, Hugh, who lived at Newton Grange, north-west of Tissington, until his death in 1524. This suggests that the monument may have been erected in the sixteenth century by Hugh Beresford's son, Laurence. The remains of the moated manor house, built by Thomas Beresford, are now part of the gabled Cherry Orchard Farm. Originally, there were two battlemented towers, but only one now survives.

PARISH CHURCH
Bradbourne

Just outside the boundary of the Peak National Park, some 5 miles north-east of Ashbourne, the tiny Domesday hamlet of Bradbourne stands on a hilltop site overlooking the valley of the Havenhill Dale Brook. The church of All Saints, dating from Anglo-Saxon times, has been considerably altered and enlarged over subsequent centuries. The square, unbuttressed west tower is Norman, together with its decorated south doorway and interior arch. In the churchyard is a repaired ninth-century preaching cross with a curious history. Apparently, before its restoration, the top portion of the shaft – split in half lengthwise – had been set up in the form of a 'V' for use as a stile. The friction of countless boots and trouser legs accounts for the fact that much of the carving has been worn smooth. The bottom half was used as a gatepost. Bradbourne Hall, near the church, dates from the late sixteenth century, and almost certainly stands on the site of the ancient manor of the Bradbournes.

HARTINGTON

Standing on the east side of the River Dove, the Derbyshire village of Hartington was recorded in the Domesday survey of 1086, and received its first recorded market charter in 1203. Most of the houses and cottages surrounding the spacious Market Place date from the eighteenth and nineteenth centuries. The Market Hall was built in 1836. In medieval times the pond or mere had a ducking stool for punishing gossips or troublemakers. The parish church of St Giles, with its perpendicular tower, dates from the early thirteenth century. It is unclear whether an earlier foundation stood on the site. The eighteenth-century gravestone of Elizabeth Barker, beside the main path, is encrusted with crinoid fossils. Hartington Hall, south-east of the church, is an excellent example of seventeenth-century Peakland vernacular architecture, with stone-mullioned windows and a gritstone-slate roof. Built by the Bateman family in 1611, it is now a Youth Hostel. The factory at the western end of the village makes Stilton cheese.

HARBORO' ROCKS
near Brassington

In the early eighteenth century Daniel Defoe visited 'Brassington Moor' and, while looking for the 'imaginary wonder' called the 'Giant's Tomb', 'found a real one': a cave inhabited by a lead-miner, his wife and five children. On enquiry, he was told that the miner had been born in the cave, and his father before him. 'There was a large hollow cave,' he wrote, 'which the poor people by two curtains hanged cross, had parted into three rooms. On one side was the chimney, and the man, or perhaps his father, being miners, had found means to work a shaft or funnel through the rock to carry the smoke out at the top ... The habitation was poor, 'tis true, but things within did not look so like misery as I expected. Every thing was clean and neat, tho' mean and ordinary.' Although some believe that the cave referred to is the one on Carsington Pasture (near the remains of the Greatrake Mine), it could equally well be the cave in Harboro' Rocks, which was also inhabited in prehistoric times.

SIGNAL BOX
Hartington

The last railway line to be built in the Peak District was the London and North Western Railway route from Buxton to Ashbourne, using part of the 33-mile High Peak Railway line from Cromford to Whaley Bridge. Although the 9-mile Buxton to Parsley Hay section of the line was completed in 1894, it was another five years before passengers could travel by train all the way to Ashbourne. After the closure of the High Peak and Ashbourne lines in the late 1960s, both routes were purchased by the Peak National Park authority and Derbyshire County Council, and converted into leisure trails for walkers, cyclists and horseriders. The High Peak Trail runs for some 17 miles from High Peak Junction, near Cromford, to Dowlow, near Buxton. At Parsley Hay it is joined by the 13-mile Tissington Trail (from Ashbourne). Many of the former stations on the two routes have been turned into car parks, while the signal box at Hartington on the Tissington Trail now serves as an information centre.

DOVEDALE
from Thorpe Cloud

Rising on the slopes of Axe Edge, 4 miles south-west of Buxton, the River Dove meanders south-eastward for some 45 miles before joining the Trent, near Stretton. The most celebrated part of its course is the deep and sinuous, 2-mile-long gorge between Milldale and Thorpe Cloud. Known as Dovedale, it has long been a popular spot. In *Rambles by Rivers: The Dove* (1845) James Thorne wrote: 'Dove-dale is the very paradise of 'gypsy-parties,' – their number is legion and their variety infinite. High-born and accomplished ladies, with well-bred gallants, and their liveried attendants, groups graceful as those delightful ones Watteau so charmingly painted – and, it must be admitted, almost as formal; pleasant family-parties, with heaps of children, and well-stored hampers, smiling papas, and staid elder daughters with their most attentive young gentlemen; merry, noisy country lots of a dozen youths and red-cheeked maidens, with one or two cheerful dames; are to be seen every bright day the summer through.'

WELL-DRESSING
Tissington

After being soaked in the village pond at Tissington, the heavy wooden frames on which the well-dressing pictures are mounted are covered with locally dug clay, mixed with water and salt to a smooth butter-soft consistency. The salt not only helps to prevent the clay from cracking by keeping it moist, it also sustains the freshness of the mosses and flowers. Most of the pictures are based on a religious theme. Once the full-sized paper design has been traced on to the clay using a pointer or toothed wheel, the painstaking task of filling in the picture is undertaken using entirely natural materials. The outlines are emphasized by pressing beans, seeds and tiny alder cones into the clay. To allow the rain to run off, each petal is inserted separately, working upward from the bottom of the picture and overlapped like tiles on a roof. Six wells are dressed at Tissington: Yew Tree Well, Hall Well, Children's Well, Hands Well, Coffin Well and Town Well.

ILAM HALL

At the beginning of the eleventh century the land at Ilam (then known as 'Hilum', meaning 'at the hills') was given to the newly founded Benedictine Abbey of Burton-upon-Trent. In 1546, after the Dissolution of the Monasteries, the estate was acquired by John Port, who built a house on the site of the present Ilam Hall. The Port family sold the estate to David Pike-Watts in 1809, and upon his death it passed to his daughter Mary. Between 1821 and 1826, her husband, Jesse Watts-Russell, a wealthy industrialist, rebuilt the house on an extravagant scale in the Gothic Revival style, with battlemented towers and ornamental chimneys. He also rebuilt the estate village of Ilam and the school. At the centre of the 'model village' is a 30-foot-high 'Eleanor' cross, erected in 1840 to honour Mary Watts-Russell. Before Sir Robert McDougall purchased Ilam Hall in 1934 and presented it to the National Trust for use as a Youth Hostel, much of the building had been demolished.

PARISH CHURCH
Wirksworth

'Wirksworth is a large well-fre-
quented market town,' wrote
Daniel Defoe in about 1725,
'though there is no very great
trade to this town but what
relates to the lead works, and to
the subterranean wretches, who
they call Peakrills, who work in
the mines, and who live all
round this town every way.'
Lead-mining has been associated
with the Wirksworth area since
at least Roman times. Indeed,
some authorities believe that the
administrative centre of the
Roman lead-mining district of
Lutudarum was sited near the
town. The Latin name has been
found stamped on pigs of lead
dug up around Matlock. A stone
carving of an Anglo-Saxon lead-
miner, carrying both pick and
kibble (a large bucket), can be
found inside the parish church of
St Mary, founded in 653.
However, the church's greatest
treasure is the 'Wirksworth
Stone', a coffin lid, elaborately
carved with scenes from the life
of Christ and thought to date
from *c*.800. The building also
contains many other carvings of
interest.

FIELD BARN
Manifold Valley

In addition to drystone walling,
so characteristic of the White
Peak landscape, many of the
upland pastures contain field
barns, used for storing hay and
sheltering animals over the winter months. (The dilapidated
barn in the photograph is near
the ruins of Throwley Hall, on
the west side of the Manifold
Valley.) Some, however, had non-
farming uses. The stone barn on
the hillside above Ecton, once
housed a Boulton and Watt
steam engine – serving the Deep
Ecton Mine by raising spoil to
the surface and pumping out
water. It is said that the mineral
wealth from this copper mine –
which reached a depth of over
1,300 feet – reaped a huge fortune for the Dukes of
Devonshire, and financed the
building of The Crescent at
Buxton. In recent times some of
the field barns have become
redundant to the farmers' needs.
Instead of being allowed to fall
into decay, a few have been converted into basic overnight
accommodation for visitors to
the Peak National Park, and are
known as 'camping barns'.

DOVEDALE CASTLE
from Bunster Hill

Many of the natural limestone rock formations in Dovedale have been given names such as Dovedale Castle, the Twelve Apostles, Tissington Spires, Ilam Rock, Raven's Tor, Reynard's Cave, Dove Holes and the Lion's Head Rock. The practice, however, was not restricted to Dovedale, as the nineteenth-century diarist James Thorne observed: 'before all the world Derbyshire stands pre-eminent in the art of naming things – every turn in every cave in the county has a name – some half a dozen – and then every thing in every compartment, to a stalagmite as big as a thimble, has one appropriated to itself.' The cliff, on the opposite side of the gorge to the Twelve Apostles, was named 'Lover's Leap' in the eighteenth century. Tradition says that after being jilted a young woman threw herself over the 130-foot precipice. Luckily, she landed in bushes, thereby cushioning her fall and saving her from death. (The peaked hill on the right in the photograph is the 942-foot-high Thorpe Cloud.)

MIDDLETON TOP
High Peak Trail

Because the construction of a navigable waterway across the high, limestone barrier of the White Peak was impractical, it was decided to link the Cromford Canal to the Peak Forest Canal with a 33-mile-long railway line. Known as the Cromford & High Peak Railway and built by Josiah Jessop (whose father, William, was the engineer of the Cromford Canal), it was finally completed in 1831. As the railway was designed like a canal, with long, level sections and short, steep inclines, the stations were known as 'wharfs'. From Cromford Wharf the line climbed almost 990 feet to reach its highest point of elevation at the top of the Hurdlow incline (1,264 feet), then fell 747 feet to Whaley Bridge. The Middleton Top Engine House, on the High Peak Trail, contains an 1829 steam winding engine, used to haul wagons up the 1 in 8 grade incline by means of chains (replaced by hemp ropes in 1856 and steel cables in 1861). It is the only engine to survive of the railway's original eight.

KEDLESTON HALL

Immediately after inheriting Kedleston in 1758, Nathaniel Curzon, 1st Baron Scarsdale, demolished the existing house and replaced it with a magnificent Palladian mansion, intending it to be a 'Temple of the Arts' for the family's collection of paintings and sculpture. By about April 1760 the original architects, Matthew Brettingham and James Paine, had been replaced by Robert Adam (1728-92), whose initial commission was simply to landscape the park and design the garden buildings. Completed in 1765, the house is especially celebrated for its beautifully co-ordinated Neo-Classical Adam interiors. Among the park buildings also designed by Adams are the elegant three-arched bridge, the North Lodge, and the Fishing Room on the Upper Lake. All that remains of the medieval village of Kedleston, which Curzon moved to the western edge of the park, is the church of All Saints. It contains many monuments to the Curzon family dating back to the thirteenth century.

MILLDALE

Situated at the northern entrance to Dovedale, the tiny hamlet of Milldale consists of only a few farms, a former mill, a chapel and a cluster of cottages, the oldest dating from the seventeenth century. One of the dwellings has been converted into a small cafe. The narrow, twin-arched, pack-horse bridge, now known as 'Viator's Bridge', was made famous by Charles Cotton in his contribution to Izaak Walton's *The Compleat Angler*. Having travelled over the hills from Ashbourne, the Viator asked: ' "What's here the sign of a Bridge? Do you use to Travel with wheel-barrows in this Country?" To which Piscator replied: "Not that I ever saw Sir, why do you ask that question?" "Because this bridge certainly was made for nothing else; why a mouse can hardly go over it: Tis not two fingers broad." ' As the River Dove forms the boundary between Staffordshire and Derbyshire, the west side of the bridge is in the former county and the east side is in the latter. Viator's Bridge is now scheduled as an ancient monument.

RIVER DOVE
Dovedale

The scenery in Dovedale has impressed and delighted many Peakland visitors. Dr Samuel Johnson (1709-84) announced that 'he who has seen Dovedale need not travel to the Highlands'. While Lord Byron (1788-1824) wrote to his friend, the Irish poet Thomas Moore (1779-1852): 'Was you ever in Dovedale? I assure you there are things in Derbyshire as noble as in Greece or Switzerland.' In addition to the spectacular limestone crags, much of the gorge is covered by natural woodland, including ash, oak, beech, rowan and wych elm. The grassland supports plants such as limestone bedstraw, Nottingham catchfly and the early purple orchid. Dippers and grey wagtails can often be seen along the famous trout and grayling river. In the past the gorge has also been noted for its local characters: particularly Annie Bennington (1869-1950) of Milldale, who had a stall below Reynard's Cave: and Billy Burton (*c.*1870-1950) or 'Donkey Billy' of Ashbourne, who ran donkey rides to and from the Stepping Stones.

SUDBURY HALL

Shortly after Charles II's restoration to the throne in 1660, George Vernon decided to transform his small manor house into one of the finest Stuart houses in England. Probably acting as his own architect, Vernon spent the next forty years adapting and improving his original ideas: partly due to his own increasing knowledge and partly due to the inspiring influence of contemporary fashions. Initially, Vernon used local craftsmen to decorate the interior, notably in the Queen's Room (named after Queen Adelaide, the wife of William IV), but by the late 1670s he was employing some of the finest craftsmen in London: Grinling Gibbons and Edward Pierce for the carving and joinery; and James Pettifer and Robert Bradbury for the plasterwork. Pierce's Great Staircase is considered to be one the finest of its kind in an English country house. The mythological scenes in the plasterwork panels were painted by Louis Laguerre. The National Trust Museum of Childhood is housed in the nineteenth-century service wing.

Matlock Bath and the Eastern Edge

EDENSOR

Chatsworth

The original village of Edensor, which stretched from the River Derwent to the site of the present church, was mostly demolished when the park at Chatsworth was landscaped by 'Capability' Brown in the 1760s. The destruction of the remaining houses east of the new turnpike road was completed by the 6th Duke of Devonshire some seventy years later. The only dwelling within the park to be spared was Park Cottage. After the construction of the two lodges (designed by Sir Jeffry Wyatville in 1837) at the northern ('Golden Gates') entrance to the park, the Duke turned his attention to rebuilding Edensor. Tradition says that when shown a book of house plans by the architect John Robertson, he quickly glanced through it, handed it back and said that he would have one of each. True or not, each house in the village – built between 1839 and 1841 – is in a different style. The present church of St Peter, retaining fragments of the old foundation, was designed by G.G. Scott for the 7th Duke, and completed in 1867.

Journeying through the Peak District in 1697 Celia Fiennes wrote:

All Derbyshire is full of steep hills ... but tho' the surface of the earth looks barren yet those hills are impregnated with rich marbles, stones, metals, iron and copper and coal mines in their bowels, from whence we may see the wisdom and benignity of our great Creator to make up the deficiency of a place by an equivalent as also the diversity of the Creation which increaseth its Beauty.

Although the minerals in the rocks were exploited during prehistoric times, the earliest evidence of mining activity in the region dates from the Roman occupation, and takes the form of around twenty ingots or pigs of smelted lead, many of which are inscribed with the letters LVT or LTVD. Most experts agree that the letters refer to the Roman lead-mining district of Lutudarum, but the precise nature and location of the place remains a matter for conjecture. Some propose that the district was centred on either Matlock or Wirksworth. Others suggest a site further north, at Chesterfield.

It is thought that the Romans extracted most of their lead ore from open-cast sites, where the larger veins or 'rakes' could be up to 60 feet wide at the surface. Whether some of the caves and mines shown to the public contain Roman workings, as is traditionally claimed, is impossible to prove because of the absence of any documentary evidence.

Anglo-Saxon references to lead production in the Peak District include the brief mention of mines owned by Repton Abbey at Wirksworth in the ninth century, and the Domesday record of what were probably smelting sites during the reign of Edward the Confessor (1042-66). The Odin Mine, near Castleton, despite being first recorded in 1280, is reputed to have received its name from having been worked during the time of the Danes. After 1288, when the lead-miners' laws and customs were first set down, mining matters were formally regulated by the 'Courts of the Barghmaster' (later known as the Small Barmote Court), held every three weeks at the mines. Its origins, however, are thought to lie in pre-Norman times: not only in the Anglo-Saxon Hundred

Courts, but also in the Danelaw Courts of King Aethelred the Unready (reigned 978-1016). The exact date of the foundation of the Great Barmote Court, which dealt with more weighty mining matters, is obscure. All that is known is that the Court was not mentioned in the *Inquisition* or *Quo Warranto* held at Ashbourne in May 1288, but was in existence by 1415.

Peakland's lead-mining industry reached the heights of production in the late eighteenth century. Despite a significant revival in demand between 1830 and 1850, mining increasingly proved to be uneconomic, mainly because of diminishing ore reserves and the cost of removing water from the workings. The final collapse of the 2,000-year-old industry was brought about by the import of cheaper foreign lead in the late nineteenth century. A few mines, like the Magpie Mine, near Sheldon, managed to continue well into the twentieth century, but most were abandoned. Today a few of the underground workings have been turned into show caves. In the Rutland Cavern (Nestus Mine) at Matlock Bath, for example, the story of a seventeenth-century lead-miner has been recreated using atmospheric sounds and special effects. While in the Speedwell Cavern, near Castleton, visitors can travel by boat along a flooded 750-yard-long subterranean passage, laboriously cut through the limestone in the eighteenth century. The Peak District Mining Museum at Matlock Bath charts the history of lead-mining in the region from Roman times. In addition to a mock-up of an old mine shaft, the exhibits include a huge water-pressure engine, dated 1819.

One of the rarest minerals found in association with lead ore is the decorative and banded variety of fluorspar known as Blue John, ranging in colour from white through deep yellow to a rich purplish blue. 'Blue John' is said either to be a corruption of the French '*bleu jaune*' (blue-yellow), or a term used by lead-miners to differentiate it from zinc blende, more commonly known as 'Black Jack'. Some locals, however, consider it to be the language uttered when someone drops a block of the stone on their foot. Nowadays, most Blue John is used to produce small trinkets and items of jewellery. In Britain the main deposits of the mineral occur to the west of Castleton, and can be found in the Blue John Cavern and the Treak Cavern, both of which are open to the public.

The limestone rock itself has been exploited since prehistoric times, not only as a building material, but as a valuable source of lime. In the construction of the baths at Aquae Arnemetiae (Buxton), for example, the Romans used mortar made with lime to cement the limestone blocks. Nevertheless, lime was mainly used as an agricultural fertilizer and most farms in the region possessed some form of kiln for burning lime-stone to produce the substance. Many of the larger industrial kilns of the nineteenth century can be found in association with quarries. For example, George Stephenson's limeworks at Ambergate, on the Cromford Canal, were linked to his limestone quar-ries at Crich by a gravity-incline, narrow-gauge railway. Another mineral worthy of note is Ashford or Black Marble, an impure form of limestone which was much in vogue for ornaments, table-tops and fire-surrounds during Victorian times. The indus-try was mainly centred on Ashford-in-the-Water, where the first marble mill was estab-lished by Henry Watson in 1748.

The coarse gritstone covering the northern, western and eastern sides of the Peak National Park was once quarried on a large scale. The stone was not only used in the construction of such famous buildings as Chatsworth House and The Crescent at Buxton, but for the manufacture of grindstones and millstones: the former for sharp-ening steel, and the latter for grinding corn. Today, below many of the 'edges', espe-cially Millstone and Stanage, are countless examples of abandoned millstones.

The abundance of water in the region may have caused the underground miners enor-mous problems, but the cotton mill-owners of the Industrial Revolution found the fast-flowing rivers to be an ideal source of power. Prior to 1771, when Richard Arkwright established the world's first successful water-powered, cotton-spinning mill at Cromford, the wool and cotton industry had been largely confined to the homes and farms of the local spinners and weavers. Arkwright not only brought mass-production methods and factory systems to the Peak, he also built one of the country's first indus-trial villages for his workers. In contravention of British law, however, the operational and technological secrets of Derbyshire's cotton-spinning industry were taken to America by Samuel Slater (1768-1835), who had worked as an apprentice in the Belper mills of Jedediah Strutt (a former partner of Arkwright). Slater now stands as a major figure in American history, and is generally regarded as the founder of the U.S. cotton textile industry.

The rich industrial heritage of the Peak District, which also includes the construc-tion of an intricate network of roads, railways and canals, not only left its mark on the landscape, it also transformed the lives and characters of the working people. Their individual stories may be forgotten, but their collective achievements are writ large in the rocks.

PARISH CHURCH
Chesterfield

Rising 228 feet above the ancient market town of Chesterfield, the octagonal spire of the parish church of St Mary and All Saints is famous for being twisted. Beneath the lead plates, laid in herringbone pattern, the timber framework is so warped and contorted that the top is some nine feet out of the vertical. The church, the largest in Derbyshire, is mainly fourteenth century, with parts like the transepts and the piers of the crossing tower dating from 1234. Its size and grandeur, together with the various chapels, reflect the wealth and piety of the medieval trade guilds which flourished in the town. The oldest, the Guild of St Mary, was founded in the early thirteenth century. When Celia Fiennes journeyed through Derbyshire in 1697, Chesterfield was a busy coal-mining and stone-quarrying centre. Lead was mined in the area as far back as Roman times. The great railway engineer, George Stephenson (1781–1848), died at Tapton House (now a school), north-east of the town. He lies buried in Holy Trinity Church.

ESTATE COTTAGE
Beeley

In Anglo-Saxon times, long before the creation of the first park at Chatsworth, there were several villages in close proximity to each other along the valley of the River Derwent, just before its confluence with the Wye. Chatsworth, standing somewhere near the site of the present Chatsworth House, and Langley, a short distance to the north, no longer exist. Edensor, its ancient church occupying the site of the present church, was partly demolished and rebuilt further to the west in the eighteenth and nineteenth centuries. Beeley, however, still retains its original location, though most of the village became part of the Chatsworth estate after its previous owners, the Saviles, died out in 1734. Some of its properties were rebuilt by Joseph Paxton for the 6th Duke of Devonshire in the mid-nineteenth century. The house in the photograph, near the Devonshire Arms, was built in 1856 by Paxton's son-in-law, G.H. Stokes. The Old Hall, thought to stand on the site of the original manor house, dates from the early seventeenth century.

CHATSWORTH HOUSE

The Derbyshire home of the Duke and Duchess of Devonshire, Chatsworth House – so-called 'Palace of the Peak' – is set in a 1,000-acre park watered by the River Derwent. The present mansion, standing on the site of Bess of Hardwick's Elizabethan house, was begun in 1687 by William Cavendish (created 1st Duke of Devonshire in 1694) and completed in 1707. To improve the view from the house, the 4th Duke demolished most of the cottages in the village of Edensor and commissioned 'Capability' Brown to landscape the garden and park. The Baroque stables were built in 1758-63 by James Paine, who also designed the bridge upstream of the house. In addition to erecting the long north wing, the 6th Duke filled the house with treasures, and entrusted the redesign of the gardens to his head gardener, Joseph Paxton (1803-65). The Emperor Fountain, built by Paxton in 1843, is the tallest in Britain. Paxton's Great Conservatory, the forerunner of the Crystal Palace (which he designed for the Great Exhibition of 1851), was demolished in 1920.

LAWRENCE FIELD
Longshaw

Covering some 1,700 acres of woodland, acid grassland and low-lying gritstone moorland, the National Trust's Longshaw Estate is centred on a former shooting lodge built in the 1820s by the 6th Duke of Rutland. Near the lodge, now converted into private flats, is a National Trust shop, restaurant and information centre. Among the landscape features of historical interest within the estate are the Bronze Age enclosures in Lawrence Field and the Sheffield Plantation, and several abandoned quarries where grindstones and millstones were produced. Stone from the Bolehill Quarry was used for the building of the Howden and Derwent Dams. A network of ancient tracks criss-cross the estate. The guidestone, dated 1709, has been moved from its original position at the meeting point of roads from Sheffield, Tideswell, Chesterfield and Hathersage. One of the best surviving relics of an ancient oak woodland in the Peak District can be found in Padley Gorge, cut by the waters of the Burbage Brook.

MILL RUINS
Chatsworth

In addition to building the stables and the bridge over the Derwent at Chatsworth for the 4th Duke of Devonshire, the architect, James Paine (1717-89), designed a new corn mill at the southern end of the park, beside the river. Built in the late 1750s, the mill ceased working in 1952. Ten years later, the building was badly damaged by two huge beech trees, brought down during a fierce storm. Instead of being demolished, however, the remains were preserved as a ruin. Paine also designed the nearby one-arched bridge, carrying the road from Edensor to Beeley. The Hunting Tower, or Stand Tower, rising above the wooded escarpment to the north-east, was built in about 1582 for Bess of Hardwick and her second husband, Sir William Cavendish. Among the many other features in the grounds at Chatsworth are: the moated Queen Mary's Bower; and the Cascade, built for the 1st Duke in 1696 and rebuilt on a grander scale five years later. The Temple or Cascade House was built in 1703.

OVERSTONES FARM
Stanage Edge

Running for over 12 miles from Derwent Edge to Chatsworth, along the eastern rim of the Derwent Valley, is a steep and almost unbroken escarpment of coarse gritstone, which includes Stanage Edge, Burbage Rocks, Froggatt Edge, Curbar Edge, Baslow Edge and Birchen Edge. Among the enclosed, upland fields below Stanage Edge are several isolated farmsteads, whose main means of livelihood are sheep and cattle farming. Most farms in the gritstone country of the Peak District lie below 700 feet. Overstones Farm, high above Hathersage, is one of the few exceptions. At more than 1,000 feet above sea level, it commands extensive views over the Derwent Valley to the limestone plateau beyond. From the legionary fort of Navio (Brough), on the banks of the Noe between Hathersage and Castleton, a Roman road climbed up Stanage Edge to continue eastward as the Long Causeway, traces of which can still be found today. In medieval times the moorland route above the edge was paved with stones to make it easier for packhorses.

PARISH CHURCH
Baslow

Originating as a river-crossing settlement beside the Derwent, Baslow was recorded in the Domesday survey of 1086 as belonging to William the Conqueror. Today, the village stands near the northern edge of Chatsworth park, and is divided into Over End, Nether End and Bridge End. At the latter, the river is spanned by a seventeenth-century, three-arched bridge, beside which is a tiny toll or guardhouse. The church of St Anne, nearby, has a broach-spired tower, supporting an unusual clockface with the name 'VICTORIA' and the date '1897' instead of numerals. In a glass case by the south door is a whip, originally used to drive trouble-some dogs out of church, and sometimes to keep the congregation in order during divine service. Some of the houses in the village belong to the Chatsworth estate. Park Lodge, a turreted, Italianate building, was erected in 1842 by John Robertson for the Duke's physician, Dr Condell. The nearby Cavendish Hotel, formerly the Peacock Inn, was enlarged in 1975, and a new wing added in 1985.

HATHERSAGE MOOR
from Burbage Rocks

From the boulder-strewn foot of the long gritstone 'edge' of Burbage Rocks, the heather- and bracken-clad Hathersage Moor slopes down towards the Derwent Valley, to end abruptly at the great rock barrier of Millstone Edge. Between Burbage Rocks and the gritstone outcrops of Higger Tor and Carl Wark is the valley of the Burbage Brook. After rising on Hallam Moors, east of Stanage Edge, and crossing Hathersage Moor – where it flows through the conifer plantation shown in the photograph and under a small packhorse bridge – the stream enters the Longshaw Estate near Burbage Bridge and the Toad's Mouth. The A625 from Sheffield descends to Hathersage by way of Burbage Bridge. At Surprise View, immediately south of Millstone Edge, the road turns sharply north-west to reveal a striking panorama of Hathersage, the Hope Valley and the High Peak. Near Grindleford Station, below Surprise View, are Padley Chapel and the ruins of Padley Hall, once owned by the Eyre family.

OX STONES
Burbage Moor

Amid the heather on Burbage Moor, above the Dark Peak 'edge' of Burbage Rocks, are a collection of gritstone boulders, known as the Ox Stones. Many of the landowners in the north, west and east of the National Park capitalize on the fact that heather is the natural habitat of the red grouse (*Lagopus lagopus scoticus*). By careful management, including controlled burning (setting light to areas of old woody heather in order to encourage new growth), the game birds are encouraged to thrive. The income received from shooting the grouse often exceeds that brought in by sheep farming. The season starts on the 'Glorious Twelfth' of August, and, on shooting days, to minimise the danger of accidents, sections of the moors are closed to the public. These areas can often be identified by the presence of turf and stone-faced shooting butts. During a single day on Broomhead Moor, southwest of Stocksbridge, in 1913, nine guns achieved a record 'bag' of 1,421.5 brace (2,843 birds).

HATHERSAGE

The church of St Michael and All Angels, dating from the fourteenth century, stands on a prominent site overlooking the former industrial centre of Hathersage. During the nineteenth century the village was noted for making needles and pins. Today it is probably most famous for the grave in the churchyard, believed to belong to Little John of the Robin Hood legend. Local tradition holds that the leader of the 'merry men' was born at Loxley, 7 miles north-east of the village, and that Little John died in the cottage which once stood to the east of Hathersage church. Apparently, the grave was opened in 1784 and found to contain a thigh bone over 30 inches long. From this, it has been estimated that the man would have been 7 feet tall. The stone in the church porch, carved with initials, is said to have originally marked the grave. Charlotte Brontë stayed at the vicarage in 1845. Her heroine in *Jane Eyre* (1847) was reputedly given the surname of the family, whose memorials are inside the church.

RIBER CASTLE

Standing high on a hill overlooking the Matlocks, Riber Castle was built in 1862 for John Smedley (1803-74), the local industrialist who did much to develop Matlock's spa, including opening the massive Hydro at Matlock Bank in 1853. With its turrets and embattled curtain walls, Pevsner considered the folly to be 'a surprising case of posthumous romanticism, due to Mr Smedley's unerring sense of publicity values'. No doubt, in addition to dominating the surrounding landscape, Smedley meant it to be seen and admired by those visiting his 'hydropathic establishment', conveniently sited on the hillside opposite. After Smedley's death, the castle remained in the family until 1888, when it was sold and became a boys' school. Closure of the school in 1930 led to the building falling into a state of disrepair. The roofless ruin is now part of the Riber Castle Wildlife Park, home of many rare breeds and endangered species, including lynx.

HIGGER TOR
from Over Owler Tor

Some 1,400 feet above sea level, Higger Tor is the most prominent of all the crags on Hathersage Moor, South Yorkshire. (In the photograph the gritstone outcrop can be seen breaking the horizon on the left. The lesser height of the flat-topped Carl Wark hillfort is in the middle distance on the right.) Popular with rock climbers, Higger Tor is famous for the huge gritstone feature known as the 'Leaning Block' or 'Leaning Tower', on which the classic route is 'The Rasp'. The block itself is 50 feet high, and overhangs more than 15 degrees from the vertical. In the middle of the escarpment is the 'Hole in the Slabs', consisting of an opening in what appears to be a pile of gritstone boulders. 'Higger', sometimes spelled 'Higgar', is thought to be a corruption of 'higher'. Scattered around the surrounding moorland are strangely shaped natural rock formations, including the Toad's Mouth, near Burbage Bridge, on which has been carved an eye.

CARL WARK
from Higger Tor

Standing on an outcrop of mill-stone grit, high on the bracken moorland east of Hathersage, are the remains of an ancient and enigmatic fortress known as Carl Wark. The rectangular enclosure, covering 2 acres, is protected on three sides by steep natural slopes, and on the western side by an artificial fortification of stone and earth. It is thought that the stronghold may have originally been encircled completely by ramparts. Although some archaeologists consider that the hillfort dates from late Iron Age, others maintain that it is Romano-British, or even post-Roman (Dark Age) in origin. John Leyland in *The Peak of Derbyshire* (1891) said that several small tumuli or burial mounds were opened at Carl Wark in 1826, but 'nothing was disclosed save deposits of burnt bones, without urns or implements of any kind, the interment may by assumed to have belonged to a very remote age'. Another tumulus on the moor, opened in 1834, revealed 'several rudely shaped and sunburnt urns, containing calcined bones'.

CRICH STAND

Occupying a prominent quarry-edge site north-west of the hilltop village of Crich, the tower, known as Crich Stand, is a landmark for miles around. At night it emits a flashing beacon light, 950 feet above sea level. One of at least three towers to stand on the limestone hill, the present 'stand' or 'view-tower' was erected in 1923 as a memorial to the men of the Sherwood Foresters regiment, who died during World War I. Its predecessor, built nearer the quarry edge in 1851, was badly damaged by lightning in 1901 and eventually demolished. The quarry was dug to provide lime for George Stephenson's kilns at Ambergate, on the Cromford Canal. Stephenson also built the gravity-incline, narrow-gauge railway that carried stone from the quarry down a 1 in 7 slope to the kilns. In 1959, two years after the railway ceased operation, the National Tramway Museum was established on the quarry site. The attractions include exhibitions, rides and about fifty trams, dating back to 1873.

HANDSTONE
Beeley Moor

On the heather-clad Beeley Moor, some 1,200 feet above sea level, are over thirty prehistoric barrows and cairns and several less-ancient wayside markers. The handstone in the photograph stands near the intersection of four roads, the north-western of which leads to Chesterfield, 7 miles distant. Although some of the old trade routes in the Peak District have been preserved as metalled roads for motor vehicles, others have almost disappeared and can only be traced by the presence of wayside crosses, milestones, snow-stones and guideposts, many of which stand in solitary isolation in the middle of nowhere. A few of the stones have been removed and used for gateposts. According to tradition, somewhere in the vicinity of the Beeley Moor Bronze Age barrow known as Hob Hurst's House (not to be confused with the rock formation of the same name in Monsal Dale) a plot was hatched to try and release Mary Queen of Scots from imprisonment at near-by Chatsworth House. It came to nothing.

WINGFIELD MANOR

Sited on a rocky hill above the River Amber, east of Crich, Wingfield Manor was built around two courtyards in the mid-fifteenth century by Ralph, 4th Lord Cromwell, Treasurer to King Henry VI and one of the richest men of his time. After Cromwell's death in 1456, the huge country mansion was purchased by John Talbot, 2nd Earl of Shrewsbury. In 1569 and 1584-85, the years in which Mary Queen of Scots was imprisoned at Wingfield, the house belonged to George Talbot, the 6th Earl of Shrewsbury, and fourth husband of Bess of Hardwick. Throughout her last brief stay at Wingfield, the queen was accompanied by more than 200 people, including yeomen, officers and soldiers. Having been partly demolished during the Civil War, the manor was sold to Immanuel Halton in 1678 and subsequently restored. His family remained in the house until 1774, after which parts of the building were dismantled to built a new manor house to the north, Wingfield Hall. The historic ruins are now in the care of English Heritage.

RIVER DERWENT AND WEIR
Belper

Prior to the arrival of the Strutt family in the eighteenth century, Belper – its name derived from the Norman-French for 'beautiful retreat' – was a small market town, on the east bank of the Derwent. Utilizing the power of the river, Jedediah Strutt (then in partnership with Richard Arkwright) built the town's first cotton mill in 1776. By the end of the century Strutt and his family had become the industrial rulers of Belper, while Arkwright ran Cromford. In addition to building eight mills, together with houses, schools, chapels and hospitals for their workers, the Strutts also developed a mill complex at Milford, a mile or so downstream. The semicircular weir at Belper, built in 1797, was designed to power a number of mill wheels by raising the level of the Derwent. Further improvements included increasing the reservoir's storage capacity in 1819. The North Mill, rebuilt in 1804 using brick, stone and iron, was one of the first fireproof mills. It now houses the Derwent Valley Visitor Centre.

NELSON'S MONUMENT
Birchen Edge

The slender monument on Birchen Edge, overlooking Baslow and the Derwent Valley, was erected in 1810 to honour Lord Horatio Nelson (1758-1805), the English admiral who won a decisive victory over the Franco-Spanish fleet at the Battle of Trafalgar, but was mortally wounded on the deck of his ship by a sniper. Nearby, three gritstone boulders, known collectively as the 'Three Ships', have been inscribed with the names 'Victory', 'Royal Soverin' (sic) and 'Defiance' (the latter has been defaced and could also read 'Reliance'). On Baslow Edge (facing Nelson's Monument across Gardom's Edge and the Bar Brook valley) is a large cross erected in 1866 to commemorate the Duke of Wellington (1769-1852), whose victory at Waterloo in 1815 brought the Napoleonic Wars to an end. Not far away is a huge solitary block of gritstone known as the Eagle Stone. According to tradition, young men from Baslow had to climb to the top of the rock to prove that they were fit for marriage. The first to formally claim the ascent, however, was J.W. Puttrell in 1900.

CURBAR EDGE

Running for over a mile from Froggatt Edge in the north to Baslow Edge in the south, Curbar Edge holds many a challenge for rock-climbing enthusiasts, with routes like 'Don't Slip Now', 'One Step Beyond', 'Homicide', 'Death on a Stick', 'Appointment with Fear' and the horrendous 60-foot wall of 'Knockin' on Heaven's Door'. In the valley below the 'edge' are the villages of Curbar and Calver, situated on the east and west banks of the Derwent, respectively. For those that remember, the cotton mill at Calver, rebuilt by Richard Arkwright in 1803-4, was turned into Colditz Castle for the BBC television series *Colditz*. From the river, a road climbs steeply through a gap in the escarpment between the 'edges' of Curbar and Baslow, and onto Big Moor, where there are extensive Bronze Age remains, including stone circles, settlement earthworks, field systems and over a hundred burial cairns. The photograph was taken from the top of Curbar Edge looking south-east to Baslow Edge and Chatsworth.

WINDMILL
Heage

Despite the abundance of water-mills (or their remains) in the Peak District, there are very few windmills. The only complete example of a tower mill in the whole of Derbyshire is the six-sailed, ogee-capped windmill at Heage, near Belper. Rebuilt after 1894, when the previous mill was severely damaged in a storm, it ceased grinding corn in 1919, and subsequently fell into disrepair. Restoration began in the 1970s, following the purchase of the mill by Derbyshire County Council. The significance of the date '1850', carved by the door, is unclear. In the late eighteenth century the scattered village of Heage (meaning 'high place') found itself in the centre of intense industrial activity – notably coal-mining and iron-smelting. In a field at Morley Park, south of Heage, are the remains of two early coke-fired blast furnaces, dating from 1780 and 1818. Built by Francis Hurt of Alderwasley Hall, Pevsner considered them to be 'the outstanding monument to the production of cast iron in Derbyshire'.

MATLOCK BATH

Although warm springs surface at Matlock Bath – one of several Matlocks strung out along the banks of the River Derwent – it is uncertain whether they were exploited by the Romans, who certainly mined lead in the area. The transformation of the village into a spa town began in 1698, when the Old Bath Hotel was built over the site of a thermal spring noted for its healing properties. However, it was not until the construction of better roads to the town in the early nineteenth century, that Matlock Bath became a fashionable place to live or to visit. The completion of the Cromford Canal in 1794 encouraged some building development, but the major expansion took place after the arrival of the railway in 1849. Today the town is a popular tourist base for the Peak National Park. Among the many attractions in the town itself are: boating on the Derwent; exploring the old caves and lead mines; riding the cable cars to the Heights of Abraham; and visiting the theme park, Gulliver's Kingdom.

MILLSTONES
Stanage Edge

Below many of the 'edges', including Stanage, Millstone and Curbar, are piles of abandoned millstones or grindstones, some roughly shaped, others almost finished. Hewn from coarse, abrasive gritstone using simple hand-tools, the labour was so exhausting that it was said 'the harder you worked the sooner you died'. The earliest form of millstone used for grinding corn dates back to prehistoric times and was known as a 'hand-mill' or 'quern'. This developed into the 'rotary quern', consisting of an upper and lower stone, the former being rotated by a stick or lever. The grain was introduced by a hole in the upper stone. By Anglo-Saxon times the quern had given way to the millstone; the larger stones being turned by animal or water power (and later wind power). Before the industry's collapse in the nineteenth century, millstones were also used for pulping wood and crushing lead ore. Grindstones were used for sharpening the products of nearby Sheffield's steel and cutlery industries.

HARDWICK HALL

After the breakdown of her marriage to the Earl of Shrewsbury, Bess of Hardwick returned to her birthplace at Hardwick, which she purchased from her brother in about 1583. Within a year or so, she began to replace the manor house with Hardwick Old Hall. In 1590, however, her husband died leaving her fabulously rich. Abandoning the Old Hall before it was even finished, Bess built an entirely new and grander house a few hundred yards away. It was to become her principal place of residence, rather than Chatsworth. Designed by Robert Smythson, the new Hardwick Hall was one of the most spectacular and innovative country houses of the Elizabethan period. The extensive use of glass, which was very expensive, gave rise to the rhyme: 'Harwick Hall, more glass than wall.' On each of the towers are Bess's initials 'E.S.' topped by a coronet. Today the house, containing outstanding tapestries and needlework, is owned by the National Trust. The ruins of the Old Hall are in the care of English Heritage.

'SALT CELLAR'
Derwent Edge

Over thousands of years, since at least the last Ice Age, the erosion of millstone grit along the 'edges' of the Peak District has produced a fascinating collection of weirdly shaped rocks or tors. Among the most distinctive are the series of gritstone outcrops on Derwent Edge. Most have been given colourful or descriptive names, such as 'Cakes of Bread', 'Hurkling Stones', and 'Wheel Stones' (alternatively known as 'Coach and Horses'). The summit of the highest, 'Back Tor', reaches 1,765 feet above sea level. In the case of the 'Salt Cellar', which stands in isolation below the crest of the ridge, the action of frost, water, wind and blown sand has removed the relatively softer layers horizontally as well as vertically. The photograph was taken looking north-west over Dovestone Clough towards the forestry plantations of the Derwent and Ladybower Reservoirs. A 'clough', incidentally, is a steep rocky valley in gritstone country; while a 'grough' is a drainage channel in peat moorland.

LEAWOOD PUMP HOUSE
Cromford Canal

As well as establishing England's first water-powered, cotton-spinning mill at Cromford in 1771, Richard Arkwright – the so-called 'Father of the Factory System' – also played a prominent role in the construction of the Cromford Canal. Although the idea of building a navigable waterway linking the unworked coalfields around Pinxton to the Erewash Canal (opened in 1779) and, thereby, the River Trent, had been mooted for some time, it was not until Arkwright's involvement in 1778 that the proposal quickly found financial and Parliamentary support. Linking Cromford to Langley Mill in the Erewash Valley (with a 2-mile branch from Ironville to Pinxton), the 14-mile-long canal was eventually opened in 1794. In addition to transporting coal, limestone, ironstone and lead, the waterway also carried cotton and yarn from Arkwright's mills. The Leawood Pump House, near High Peak Junction, was built in 1849 to pump water from the River Derwent into the canal.

HARDWICK OLD HALL

Incorporating fragments of an earlier house, Hardwick Old Hall was essentially built between 1585 and 1590 by Elizabeth, Countess of Shrewsbury, more famously known as Bess of Hardwick (1527-1608). The Hardwicks, a family of the minor gentry, had lived on the site since the fourteenth century. When Bess's father died in 1528, she only received a small amount of money. In fact, the family were left almost in poverty. Yet by the time of her death, Bess had become, through four marriages, one of the wealthiest women in England. Her first husband, Robert Barlow (or Barley), was also her cousin. He died shortly after their marriage in about 1543 leaving her a comfortable sum, but not a fortune. The only husband by which she had children was the elderly Sir William Cavendish, son of Thomas Cavendish of Suffolk. After his death in 1557, Bess married Sir William St Loe (d. 1565) and finally the immensely rich George Talbot, 6th Earl of Shrewsbury (c.1528-90), one of the most powerful men in the country.

BOOT'S FOLLY
Bradfield Moor

Standing on a prominent height overlooking Bradfield Moors, Boot's Folly was built in 1927 to provide work for the unemployed. Named after Charles Boot of nearby Bents House, the 55-foot-high tower was inspired by a similar folly on Ughill Moor, and constructed using stone from demolished buildings. It was upon the moorland hereabouts – at 'Whitcross' – that Jane Eyre, in Charlotte Brontë's book of the same title (first published in 1847) was set down by the coachman after fleeing from 'Thornfield Hall'. The 'stone pillar set up where four roads meet' is thought by some to be Moscar Cross, a mile or so south of Boot's Folly. Others, however, locate it near the Fox House Inn, above Longshaw. 'Moor House', where Jane found refuge after nearly perishing on the moors, is said to be Moorseats, north-east of Hathersage. The nearby North Lees Hall was Mr Rochester's 'Thornfield Hall'. Tradition says that, like Mrs Rochester, its first mistress went mad and died in a fire.

PARISH CHURCH
Bradfield

Located just inside the Peak National Park, north-west of Sheffield, the village of Bradfield contains several places of interest including the church of St Nicholas, a watch-house and the earthwork remains of a Norman motte-and-bailey castle. The latter, on Bailey Hill, is one of two ancient fortifications situated in close proximity, both of which are now scheduled as national monuments. The gargoyled church, in High Bradfield, dates mainly from the fifteenth century. It contains an Anglo-Saxon cross, embellished with five half-balls, that was found in a field at Low Bradfield in 1870. The tiny crypt with a fireplace, known as the Sunken Vestry, was used by visiting priests from Ecclesfield Priory (north of Sheffield). At the graveyard gates of the church (and shown in the photograph) is the Watch-house, built in 1745 for a nightly guard who was employed to prevent body-snatching. In 1864 the dam of the Dale Dike Reservoir collapsed drowning almost 250 people, some of whom lived in Low Bradfield.

Bakewell and the Central Peak

Huddled together on the lime-stone plateau south of Sheldon are the remains of the Magpie Mine, one of the best preserved and most impressive lead mines in the Peak District. The buildings, now in the care of the Peak District Mines Historical Society, date from the nineteenth century and include the mine agent's house and adjacent smithy, a Cornish beam engine house with a round chimney, and the square chimney of a winding engine house, of which only the winding drum and drive shaft remain. The 728-foot-deep main shaft is flooded to a depth of about 150 feet. Although lead extraction in the area dates back to at least Roman times, it was during the eighteenth and nineteenth centuries that the industry reached its peak. Decline set in after the import of cheaper foreign lead in the 1870s, and by 1900 nearly all of the mines had been abandoned. The Magpie Mine was formally closed in 1924, but lead continued to be extracted on a small scale until the 1950s. Tradition says that the mine is cursed.

According to legend, in September 1501 Arthur, Prince of Wales and eldest son of King Henry VII, was exploring the countryside around Bakewell and on reaching the crossroads, just over a mile south of the village of Hassop, decided to rest under an ancient cross. At the time, the fifteen-year-old heir to the English throne was staying at Haddon Hall, the home of his governor and treasurer, Sir Henry Vernon. He was also betrothed to Catherine of Aragon, the daughter of Ferdinand and Isabella of Spain. Falling asleep beneath the cross, the prince dreamt of a woman in white who prophesied that he would die shortly after his future wife landed on British soil. Returning to Haddon, he was informed that Catherine would shortly be arriving at Plymouth from Spain, and that they were to be married at St Paul's Cathedral in November. Just as the vision foretold, a little over four months after the wedding the prince fell ill and died. Tradition says that his last words were: 'O, vision of the cross at Haddon' The cross, dating from the ninth century and decorated with vine scrolls, animals and human figures, now stands in All Saints' churchyard at Bakewell. The widowed Catherine of Aragon, of course, eventually married Arthur's younger brother, King Henry VIII.

The old market town of Bakewell is just one of many places in the Peak District where history, legend and folklore have become closely linked. At Eyam, for example, the epic sacrifice of the villagers during the plague of 1665-66 has not only become a legend in itself, it has also given rise to a collection of stories about ghosts and strange events. The supposed spectre of Catherine Mompesson, the wife of the rector and one of the victims of the plague, is said to haunt the Rectory. While a notice over the door of the Miners' Arms Inn claims that it is 'reputed to be one of the most haunted houses in the village'. One ghost, seen dressed in boots, bonnet and cape, is thought to be the murdered wife of a former landlord. On his inebriated way home from another of the village's pubs, Tom Cockeye, a nineteenth-century lead-miner, encountered the phantom of Eyam Dell. Apparently, the experience was so terrifying that he made a life-long vow never to drink alcohol again.

Lud's Church, near the Roaches, is reputed to be haunted by Alice, the granddaughter of Walter de Ludauk, whose body was buried at the entrance to the deep rocky ravine in the early fifteenth century. At the time of the girl's death, the chasm was being used for secret worship by the Lollards, followers of the religious reformer John Wyclif (or Wycliffe). Ludauk, in fact, was conducting the service, while Alice was among the congregation. Unfortunately, their fervent singing was heard by passing soldiers and in the ensuing fight, the young girl was killed. Although some of the Lollards managed to escape, Ludauk was captured and died in captivity. For many years, until it was destroyed by vandals, the ship's figurehead of a young woman stood in the ravine as a tribute to the slain girl. Allegedly, in addition to being the legendary Green Chapel of the medieval poem *Sir Gawain and the Green Knight*, Lud's Church is also reputed to have been one of Robin Hood's many hiding places. Tradition says that the celebrated outlaw was born at Loxley, north-west of Sheffield, while Little John was buried at Hathersage. The gravestone of 'the friend and lieutenant of Robin Hood' states that he 'died in a cottage (now destroyed) to the east of the churchyard'.

Scattered throughout the region are countless graves, plaques and memorial stones, many of which bear inscriptions about people and incidents that otherwise may have been forgotten. The devotion of Tip the sheepdog, for example, is commemorated by a memorial close to the Derwent Dam. Apparently, through the severe winter of 1953-54, the dog spent fifteen weeks on Howden Moor keeping watch over the dead body of her master, Joseph Tagg. The terse and enigmatic inscription 'M. Hyde 1664', on one of the stone bridges at Ashford-in-the-Water, refers to the death of the Reverend Hyde, who drowned in the river after being thrown over the parapet from his horse. Conversely, a gravestone in Longnor churchyard bears the following extended epitaph:

In memory of William Billinge, who was born in a cornfield at Fawfieldhead in this parish in the year 1679. At the age of 25 years he enlisted into His Majesty's Service under Sir George Rooke and was at the taking of the fortress of Gibraltar in 1704. He afterwards served under the Duke of Marlborough at the ever memorable battle of Ramillies, fought on the 23rd of May, 1706, where he was wounded by a musket shot in the thigh. He afterwards returned to his native country and with manly courage defended his Sovereign's rights at the Rebellion in 1715 and 1745. He died within the space of 150 yards of where he was born, and was interred here the 30th of January, 1791, aged 112 years.

The 'Rebellion' referred to involved the Jacobites, supporters of the deposed King of England, James II, and his heirs. Both uprisings failed. In the 1745 rebellion led by Charles Edward Stuart, better known as Bonnie Prince Charlie, the Jacobite army invaded England from Scotland and managed to reach Derby. Finding that the English would not rally to his support, 'the Young Pretender' was forced to retreat northwards. His army was overwhelmingly defeated at the battle of Culloden in April 1746. Charles fled and was sheltered by his faithful followers for some five months until he was able to escape to France. He died in Rome on 30 January 1788, a lonely and embittered drunkard. Various battles fought during World War II are commemorated on tablets erected around the base of the celebrated yew tree in St Helen's churchyard, Darley. The tree itself is said to be over 1,000 years old. Probably the most famous memorial in the Peak District is the bronze plaque which was unveiled at Bowden Bridge Quarry, Hayfield, on 24 April 1982 to mark the fiftieth anniversary of the 'Mass Trespass' on Kinder Scout in 1932.

In addition to historical events, conspicuous topographical features have influenced the folklore and legends of the Peak, especially with regard to stories about the supernatural. The Nine Ladies Stone Circle on Stanton Moor, for instance, are said to be nine maidens who were turned to stone for dancing on the Sabbath. The Devil, it seems, was responsible for twisting the spire on the parish church at Chesterfield. And Hob's House, a landslip in Monsal Dale, is reputed to be the home of a giant, endowed with great and mysterious powers. Many of the underground caverns and mines were also thought to be inhabited by supernatural creatures, especially fairies, goblins and elves. It appears that Eldon Hole, near Peak Forest, was not simply one of Charles Cotton's 'Seven Wonders of the Peak', it was also believed to be an entrance into the infernal regions. Tradition says that in the sixteenth century a man was lowered down on a rope into the pothole to find out whether it was bottomless or not. After his screams had alerted those on the surface to the fact that something terrible had happened, he was pulled up and found to be insane. He died shortly afterwards.

The legends, folklore and traditions of the Peak District are as much a part of the region's geographical position and history as they are of the life and character of its people. As Defoe wrote in about 1725, 'the Peak people are mighty fond of having strangers shown everything they can, and of calling everything a wonder'. Yet, on his own admission, the search for an imaginary wonder, can sometimes lead to a real one.

VILLAGE CROSS
Wheston

The old farming settlement of Wheston stands high on the limestone plateau, north-east of Buxton. At the western end of the hamlet is a rare example of a complete fifteenth-century cross with carved representations of the Crucifixion and the Nativity. It is thought to have originally been a boundary cross of the former Royal Forest of the Peak. At the opposite end of the hamlet is the base of a wayside cross, known locally as the 'Wishing Stone'. In addition to various longhouse-type farm buildings, designed to shelter people and livestock under a single roof, Wheston is noted for its eighteenth-century Hall, with parts dating from the late sixteenth and seventeenth centuries. Tradition says that the house is haunted by several ghosts, including the spectre of a lady wearing a nightgown, who moves barefoot through the rooms, shrieking and tearing her golden hair. It is said that the woman, together with her lover, who lived at the Hall, murdered the husband and buried his body in the orchard.

HADDON HALL

One of the finest medieval houses in England, Haddon Hall – the Derbyshire seat of the Duke of Rutland – stands on a limestone outcrop above the River Wye. Dating from the twelfth century, with even earlier fragments, the house was altered and extended over subsequent centuries. From 1641, when the 1st Duke of Rutland moved the family's main residence to Belvoir Castle in Leicestershire, the property stood empty. Although it was not entirely neglected, its abandonment for almost 300 years ensured that the structure escaped any changes which may have been brought about by the whims of architectural fashion. The 9th Duke, who returned to Haddon at the beginning of the twentieth century, carefully restored the house to its original condition. In addition to the terraced gardens, the house is noted for its tapestries, wood carvings and wall paintings. The small iron manacle and lock, attached to a wooden screen in the Banqueting Hall, was used to punish guests 'who did not drink fayre'.

ASHFORD-IN-THE-WATER

On the River Wye, two miles upstream of Bakewell, Ashford-in-the-Water was a centre of the 'Black Marble' industry in the eighteenth and nineteenth centuries. During Victorian times the mineral was in vogue for ornaments, vases, brooches and fireplace-surrounds. A fine table-top, inlaid with the 'marble', can be found in the church of Holy Trinity. The building – almost completely rebuilt in 1869 – also preserves several historic funeral garlands, made for young girls who died unmarried. Known as Virgin Crants or Maiden's Garlands, they were carried into the church after the burial ceremony and hung from the beams above the pews. The earliest is to Anne Howard who died on 12 April 1747, aged twenty-one. The last was carried for Elizabeth Blackwell, thought to have drowned in the river in 1801. The oldest of Ashford's bridges is the medieval 'Sheepwash Bridge', originally built for packhorses, and named after the adjacent stone enclosure once used for washing sheep.

HIGHLOW VALLEY
from Over Owler Tor

Rising on Abney Moor, the waters of the Bretton Brook flow north-eastward from Great Hucklow, through the steep-sided valley of Bretton Clough, to meet a smaller stream from Abney Clough at Stoke Ford. From here the river becomes the Highlow Brook and, after journeying a further 3 miles down the Highlow Valley, enters the Derwent near Leadmill Bridge, Hathersage. (The wooded valley can be seen in the photograph, separating Eyam Moor on the left from Offerton Moor on the right. The Derwent Valley, running horizontally right to left, is hidden below the foreground rocks of Over Owler Tor.) In 1745, when the Jacobite army of 'Bonnie Prince Charlie' invaded Derbyshire, the Eyam farmers hid their cattle in Bretton Clough. Cockey Farm, midway between Bretton Clough and Abney, is the birthplace of William Newton (1750-1830), the carpenter-poet known as the 'Minstrel of the Peak'. Highlow Hall, probably dating from the late sixteenth century, was built by the powerful Eyre family who owned much land in the area.

MONYASH

Nestling in a hollow, high on the limestone uplands near the head of Lathkill Dale, the ancient farming village of Monyash was once an important lead-mining centre, with its own Barmote Court for settling the miners' disputes. Built of local limestone, the houses are mainly eighteenth and early nineteenth century. On the green, near the seventeenth-century Bull's Head inn, are the remains of the market cross, dating from 1340 when the village received its market charter. The pond, known as Fere Mere, is fed by an underground spring and was once used by the villagers as a source of drinking water, and for watering cattle. Originally there were five, but only Fere Mere survives. Inside the parish church of St Leonard, dating from the late twelfth century, are several items of interest, including a Norman piscina (stone basin) and sedilia (three seats for the clergy). The large iron-bound oak chest is thought to be fourteenth century. The church spire was rebuilt in the major restoration of 1886-88.

ROCK BASIN
Eyam Moor

When the bubonic plague came to Eyam in August 1665 a few of the villagers, like Andrew Merrill, abandoned their homes and, while honouring their self-imposed quarantine by remaining inside the parish boundary, camped for the duration on Eyam Moor. Had it been known that the disease was transmitted to humans by the bites of fleas which had previously fed on infected rats, all the villagers would have been advised to do the same, and the number of deaths would have been dramatically reduced. Sadly, at the time the means by which the plague spread was unknown. High on the heather-clad moorland are several natural rock basins, often filled with water. Although not used for the purpose, they serve as a poignant reminder that payment for the provisions that were left at specific boundary points for the villagers, was often 'disinfected' by being placed in running water or vinegar. Stones drilled with holes especially for the purpose were known as 'penny stones' or 'vinegar stones'.

ARBOR LOW STONE CIRCLE

High on Middleton Common, 3 miles west of Youlgreave, are several prehistoric sites including the Neolithic Arbor Low Stone Circle and the Bronze Age Gib Hill round barrow. The former, known as the 'Stonehenge of Derbyshire', is considered to be the most important prehistoric monument in the Peak District. Surrounded by a ditch and bank, some 250 feet in diameter, the circle is formed by over forty massive, recumbent limestone slabs, which were originally upright. It is estimated that the 6-foot-deep ditch, cut in solid limestone, would have taken fifty people six months to dig. The feat is even more remarkable when it is realized that some of the boulders in the bank weigh almost a ton. The three fallen stones lying in the centre of the circle formed part of a 'cove', possibly used for astronomical observations. The burial mound at Gib Hill, built on the site of a Neolithic long barrow, is linked to the circle by a ridge of earth. A gallows stood on the hill in more recent times.

ROBIN HOOD'S STRIDE

Robin Hood's Stride – the distinctive gritstone outcrop on Harthill Moor, west of Birchover – is topped by two fluted pinnacles, known to rock climbers as the Weasel and Inaccessible. Considering the distance between the pinnacles is over 60 feet, it is difficult to imagine that the outlaw could have jumped, let alone strode across the gap. Its alternative name, Mock Beggar's Hall, is thought to have arisen from the fact that travellers on the ancient Portway track could have easily mistaken it for a house or castle where they could beg food. During the eighteenth century, the rocks (like others in the area) were thought to have been used by the Druids for the performance of their religious rites. In *Gem of the Peak* (1851) William Adam wrote that the tor had 'the appearance of rocks still exposed to the action of water and the rolling in of heavy seas, which fret and foam through their rents and hollows at every tide, and dash their spray over their loftiest pinnacles'.

NINE STONES
Harthill Moor

On Harthill Moor – west of Stanton Moor (an important Bronze Age ritual site and burial ground) – are the remains of a stone circle, thought to have originally been some 45 feet in diameter. Dating from about 1600 to 1000 BC, the Bronze Age monument consists of four upright stones, whose only use today seems to have been downgraded to rubbing posts for cattle. Excavation of the most southerly stone revealed it to be over 11 feet long, of which 4-and-a-half feet was buried below ground. Tradition says that there were originally nine stones, one of which may be found in the stone wall to the south. The whereabouts of the rest is unknown. Hidden amid the trees of the nearby Cratcliffe Rocks is a shallow cave with a crucifix, over 3 feet high, carved in the rock. There is also a carved rock seat and a niche for a lamp. Reputed to have been occupied by a medieval hermit, the cave is now protected by iron railings.

THE MIRES
Birchover

The tradition that the Rowtor Rocks at Birchover, north of Winster, were used for druidical practices is reflected in the name of the nearby Druid Inn. In the early eighteenth century the Reverend Thomas Eyre of Rowtor Hall carved passages, rooms, steps and rough seats in the gritstone rocks. At the eastern end of the ridge is a huge 'rocking stone', weighing some 80 tons, which was once so delicately poised that it could be rocked by a single hand. In 1799, however, fourteen youths managed to push it off its pivot, and, although the stone was replaced, the balance could not be restored. Inside Rev. Eyre's chapel (now church), below the rocks and next to the Old School, are a remarkable collection of wood carvings and wall paintings. The houses on the right in the photograph (taken from Rowtor Rocks) stand below Eagle Tor at the north-western end of Birchover. The village with the pinnacled church tower, beyond Carrs Wood, is Youlgreave. Over Haddon lies on the hillside to the right.

NINE LADIES STONE CIRCLE

Among the seventy or so prehistoric barrows and cairns on Stanton Moor is an Early Bronze Age stone circle known as the Nine Ladies. Consisting of nine small gritstone boulders, the 50-foot-diameter circle stands on a low rubble bank with entrance gaps to the north-east and south-west. Tradition says that they are nine women who were turned into stone for dancing on the Sabbath. The isolated King Stone, standing some 90 feet to the south-west, is said to be the fiddler. Excavations have revealed that the moorland plateau was an Early Bronze Age burial ground. From the over eighty cremations found in some twenty cairns, it has been estimated that between 300 and 400 people were buried in the area. In the eighteenth century there were at least three more stone circles in the vicinity, but these have been destroyed. The square tower nearby was erected in honour of Earl Grey (1764-1845), the Prime Minister who steered the Reform Act of 1832 through parliament despite fierce opposition.

CHELMORTON

At over 1,200 feet above sea level, Chelmorton is the highest village in Derbyshire. Strung out along a single street and sheltered by the 1,474-foot-high Chelmorton Low, the cottages and farmhouses are surrounded by a network of limestone walling, based on the long, narrow fields of medieval strip farming. Having cleared the surface of the ground, the villagers used the stones to enclose what was once one large open field. Most of the long, narrow fields, laid out at right angles to the street, are the same width as the street frontage of a single farmstead. The larger rectangular fields, further away from the settlement, were walled after the Enclosure Awards of 1809. At the top of the street, tucked under the Low, stands the medieval church of St John the Baptist, noted for its ancient coffin stones and rare fifteenth-century chancel screen. The quaintly named Illy Willy Water emerges above the church, then almost immediately disappears to continue its journey through the village underground.

'CATHEDRAL OF THE PEAK'
Tideswell

Known as the 'Cathedral of the Peak' because of its size and grandeur, the parish church of St John the Baptist at Tideswell was built almost entirely in the Decorated style of the fourteenth century. The tower and west window, last to be built, are perpendicular. Much of the money for its construction, interrupted by the Black Death, was provided by the wealthy Foljambe and Meverell families. The brass in the chancel to John Foljambe, who died in 1358, is a copy made in 1875. The original was lost or stolen. Nearby, is a brass to Robert Pursglove (1504-79), Bishop of Hull, who founded the grammar school in 1560. The large tomb in the middle of the chancel belongs to Sir Sampson Meverell, a veteran of the Hundred Years' War with France, who died in 1462. Many of the wood carvings in the church are by the local Victorian craftsman, Advent Hunstone. In medieval times Tideswell – strung out along a dry valley on the limestone plateau – was a thriving market town and lead-mining centre.

MONSAL DALE VIADUCT

In 1863, when the Monsal Dale Viaduct was built to carry the Midland Railway's main line from London to Manchester, John Ruskin protested: 'The valley is gone and the Gods with it, and now every fool in Buxton can be at Bakewell in half an hour and every fool in Bakewell at Buxton; which you think a lucrative process of exchange – you Fools everywhere.' In addition to carrying freight, which included taking local goods to the cities, the line brought an influx of visitors to the Peak. In 1980, twelve years after the Peak section of the line closed, the track was purchased by the National Park, who converted it into the 8-and-a-half mile Monsal Trail footpath, linking Coombs Road Viaduct (southeast of Bakewell) to Wyedale (east of Buxton). Because several tunnels along the route had to be closed for safety reasons, alternative paths were created. Despite the controversy over the building of the viaduct, it is now considered to be a feature worthy of historic and architectural interest.

RIVER WYE
Monsal Dale

From its source on the gritstone
moorlands west of the Georgian
spa town of Buxton, the River
Wye cuts a south-westerly course
through limestone country to
Rowsley (south of Chatsworth),
where it joins the Derwent – a
tributary of the Trent. Near the
hamlet of Little Longstone, some
3 miles north-west of Bakewell,
the river flows under the stone
arches of the Monsal Dale
Railway Viaduct and past the
natural rock formation, known
as Hob's House (beneath which
is the weir in the photograph).
Legend says that Hob was a giant
who emerged at night to thresh
the corn of the local farmers,
who, in turn, rewarded him with
a bowl of cream. For centuries
the river's energy has been har-
nessed to operate water mills,
though most are now derelict. In
addition to building England's
first water-powered, cotton-
spinning mill on the Derwent at
Cromford, near Matlock, in
1771, Richard Arkwright established two more on the Wye:
Lumford Mill at Bakewell and
Cressbrook Mill in Water-cum-
Jolly-Dale.

YOULGREAVE

Running along the limestone
ridge above the River Bradford,
three miles south of Bakewell, is
the former lead-mining village of
Youlgreave (locally known as
Pommie). Dominating the
ancient market settlement is the
tall perpendicular tower of the
partly Norman church of All
Saints. Its unique, twelfth-
century font originally belonged
to the church of All Saints at
Elton, a few miles to the south,
but was discarded in 1838.
When the Elton parishioners
asked for it back, Youlgreave
presented them with a replica.
Projecting from the mouth of a
salamander, on the side of the
font, is a small bowl or stoup.
Edward Burne-Jones designed the
glass in the east window. The
alabaster effigy of Thomas
Cockayne (d.1488), on the tomb
in the chancel, is only 3-and-a-
half feet in length; not because he
was small, but because he died
young (killed in a fight). Near
Youlgreave's stone water tank,
known as 'The Fountain' and
dated 1829, is a small dwelling
known as 'Thimble Hall'.

ALPORT
near Youlgreave

At the confluence of the rivers Bradford and Lathkill, Alport was once surrounded by intensive lead-mining activity. Most of the cottages were built in the seventeenth and eighteenth centuries when the industry was at its height. The eighteenth-century corn mill (shown in the photograph) is now a private residence. Before the introduction of effective pumping equipment, drainage soughs were dug to lower the water table in the mines. Work on Hillcarr Sough, the longest in Derbyshire at 4-and-a-half miles, began in 1766 and took twenty-one years to complete. It ran underground from the workings at Alport to the west bank of the River Derwent, near Darley Dale. On the hillside downstream of Alport are the remains of a nineteenth-century lead-smelting works. Here the ore was smelted in coal-fired reverberatory 'cupola' furnaces, and the poisonous vapour channelled through long condensing flues before being released into the atmosphere by way of a tall chimney.

TANSLEY DALE
near Litton

One of the most characteristic features of the White Peak landscape is the intricate network of pale limestone walling, often standing out in stark contrast to the green of the fields. It has been estimated that in the limestone area of the National Park alone there are some 26,000 miles of drystone walls. Like those at Chelmorton, the walls surrounding Litton (including those running down to Tansley Dale) are based on the medieval open-field system of strip farming. Most of the walls were built as a direct result of the Enclosure Acts of the eighteenth and nineteenth centuries, but some were erected by agreement much earlier. Indeed, it has been established that a few of the walls in the National Park are Roman in origin. Although the repair and maintenance of the walls is one of the least concerns of the hard-pressed hill farmer, the Park authority tries to assist through farm management grants, and by providing volunteers and training in the ancient craft.

RIVER LATHKILL
near Conksbury

Rising from deep-seated springs among the limestone crags east of Monyash, the waters of the River Lathkill flow eastward through mixed woodland and under the medieval bridge at Conksbury to join the Bradford at Alport. During drier periods, the water in the upper reaches often disappears underground. In wet weather, however, the river's primary source is in Lathkill Head Cave. Above Conksbury Bridge and near the site of a deserted medieval settlement, the river cascades over a series of small weirs, built to improve fish stocks. As it is not contaminated by acidic soils, like most upland streams, the Lathkill is one of the purest limestone rivers in England. In the second part of Izaak Walton's *The Compleat Angler* (1676) Charles Cotton considered the Lathkill to be 'by many degrees, the purest, and most transparent stream that I ever saw either at home or abroad, and breeds, 'tis said, the reddest, and the best trouts in England'. In 1972 over 120 acres of woodland in the dale was created a National Nature Reserve.

RILEY GRAVES
Eyam

When the plague came to Eyam in 1665, borne in a box of cloth or clothes from London, the rector, William Mompesson, persuaded the villagers to quarantine themselves within the parish and thereby prevent the disease from spreading further. Although some families left, the majority remained, knowing that their chances of survival were very slim indeed. When the terrible infection extinguished itself fourteen months later, over 250 people had died. One of the last to succumb was Mompesson's wife, Catherine. In a letter to his patron, Sir George Savile, the rector wrote that 'had she loved herself as well as me, she had fled from the pit of destruction with her sweet infants, and might have prolonged her days. But she was resolved to die a martyr for my interest'. In the Riley Graves, east of the village, are Elizabeth Hancock's husband and six children, whom she buried during eight days in August 1666. The graves are now in the care of the National Trust.

PARISH CHURCH
Bakewell

Standing on high ground to the west of Bakewell, the parish church of All Saints has an octagonal tower and spire, rebuilt in 1841-52 when the twelfth- to fourteenth-century building was much restored. Fragments of Anglo-Saxon work, together with a ninth-century cross in the churchyard, indicate the presence of a pre-Conquest foundation on the site. The nearby Old House Museum, dating from 1534, contains items of local history, including memorabilia relating to Arkwright, who built the Bakewell (Lumford) cotton mill in 1778. The seventeenth-century Market Hall in the heart of the town is now an information centre for the Peak District National Park. According to tradition, an error at a local inn gave birth to the celebrated Bakewell Pudding. In about 1860 the cook, when asked to prepare a strawberry tart, mistakenly poured the egg mixture over the jam, instead of mixing it into the pastry. The result was so popular that several bakeries in the town now make rival claims to the original, secret recipe.

LATHKILL DALE
near Ricklow Quarry

Near the head of Lathkill Dale, with its limestone crags and slopes of scree, is Ricklow Quarry, worked until about 1900 for the dark polished limestone known locally as 'Black Marble'. Near the quarry is the entrance to a small lead mine, dug by Isaac Beresford in 1787. In fact, lead-mining in the dale dates back at least to medieval times, with 1288 being the earliest documented date. Among the lead-mining remains are: the ruins of the engine house of the Mandale Mine, built in 1847; and the derelict Bateman's House, named after an agent of the Lathkill Mine. The limestone piers, near the Mandale Mine, were part of an aqueduct, erected in about 1840 to carry water to the mine from Cow Gate Pool, about a mile upstream. Both the Lathkill and Mandale mines were at their peak between 1760 and 1850, but had ceased working by 1865. Not far from the foundations of Carter's (corn) Mill, is a small waterfall known as the Tufa Dam ('tufa' being a porous reconstituted stone formed by deposits of limestone).

PETER'S STONE
Cressbrook Dale

Dominating the head of Cressbrook Dale – a tributary valley of the River Wye, east of Litton – is a large, detached block of limestone, known as Peter's Stone. The dale is reputed to be haunted by the ghost of Anthony Lingard of Tideswell, who was hung from a gibbet on Peter's Stone in 1815, having been convicted of the brutal murder of a toll-bar keeper at the nearby hamlet of Wardlow Mires. Indeed, certain individuals, while taking a rest in the vicinity, have reported the sensation of being strangled by invisible hands. Further south, the windswept grassland gives way to sheltered woods. As the dale supports an unrivalled variety of plant species, it is botanically one of the most important in the the Peak District. Cressbrook Mill, at the foot of the dale, was first built by Richard Arkwright in or about 1783. It burnt down in 1785 and was rebuilt in 1814. The section of the Wye, immediately upstream of the mill, is quaintly known as Water-cum-Jolly-Dale.

VILLAGE GREEN
Foolow

Centred around a crossroads, green and pond, the small, compact, upland village of Foolow lies two miles west of Eyam. Its medieval cross originally stood near the Wesleyan Reform chapel, but was resited on the green in 1868. The nearby stone, with its iron ring, was used to tether bulls while they were set upon for sport by the villagers' dogs. Bullbaiting was made illegal in 1835. The walled pond, or mere, is fed by an underground spring and was formerly used for watering cattle. At one time there were five inns in the village. The only one to survive is the Bull's Head Inn. The Spread Eagle House, formerly an inn, retains its tethering rings for horses. Most of the houses date from the eighteenth and nineteenth centuries. The manor house and the Old Hall were both built in the seventeenth century. Like the chapel, the tiny church of St Hugh was erected in the nineteenth century. Its porch was added in 1928 using stone from the old smithy.

PARISH CHURCH
Eyam

The parish church of St Lawrence in the 'Plague Village' of Eyam is largely fourteenth and fifteenth century, with fragments dating from Norman times. Although it is uncertain whether an Anglo-Saxon foundation stood on the site, the Celtic or Saxon Cross in the churchyard – depicting the Madonna and Child – suggests that Christian worship was established in the area by the eighth or ninth century. The cross, however, does not stand on its original site. Some suggest that it was first erected on Cross Low, west of the village; others, that it stood at Wet Withens on Eyam Moor to the north. Unfortunately, part of the shaft is missing. The curious sundial on the south wall of the church dates from 1775, and is marked with signs of the zodiac and place names (like London, Bermuda, Jerusalem and Mecca). The first victim of the bubonic plague, which wiped out most of the villagers, died at Plague Cottage, near the church, on 7 September 1665. The second victim died in the same house fifteen days later.

EYAM HALL

Opposite the village stocks and late nineteenth-century Market Hall, west of the parish church, Eyam Hall was built of millstone grit by Thomas Wright in 1676 – ten years after the plague had claimed its last victim in the village. The house, with its family portraits, tapestries and Jacobean staircase, still belongs to the Wright family and is open to the public at certain times. Bradshaw Hall, now in ruins, was abandoned when the plague broke out in 1665. Many of the cottages in the former lead-mining, cotton-spinning and silk-weaving village bear plaques with information about the occupants who remained, and died, in their self-imposed quarantine. As no one could leave or enter the village, provisions were left at agreed points on the parish boundary: one being Mompesson's Well, to the north, and another the Boundary Stone, to the east. As a precaution, the church was closed and services held in the open air at Cucklett Delf, a deep, natural hollow south-west of Eyam Hall.

Buxton and the Western Moors

BIDDULPH GRANGE GARDEN

Originally laid out between 1846 and 1871 by the wealthy industrialist, James Bateman, (together with his wife, Maria, and the marine artist, Edward Cooke), the spectacular 15-acre gardens at Biddulph Grange have been meticulously restored by the National Trust, using a variety of references including old photographs. The garden, now considered to be the most complete high-Victorian garden in England, has been divided into a series of areas, with paths, tunnels, terraces, rock-work, tree-stumps and small buildings. Designed as settings for a wide variety of plants from all over the world, they include: The Italian Garden; The Pinetum; The Rhododendron Ground; Egypt; The Dahlia Walk; and China, with its 'willow-pattern' bridge and brightly coloured pagoda. Elements of humour and surprise contribute to the garden's unusual and distinctive character. The house, rebuilt after a fire in 1896, was converted into a hospital in 1923. It was bought by the National Trust in 1988.

Two of the so-called Seven Wonders of the Peak (St Ann's Well and Poole's Hole or Cavern) are located in Buxton. Occupying a hollow at the southern extremity of the Pennines – where limestone meets gritstone – the Derbyshire market town is one of the highest in England at over 1,000 feet above sea level. The waters of St Ann's Well, like all of Buxton's thermal springs, emerge from their underground source at a constant temperature of 28°C or 82°F. Recognizing the healing properties of the natural springs, the Romans established a settlement on the site, calling it Aquae Arnemetiae, meaning the 'waters of Arnemetia, the goddess of the sacred grove'. Their baths, filled with water from the springs, were lined with locally mined lead. After the withdrawal of the legions from Britain in the early fifth century, however, the wells were abandoned and the buildings allowed to fall into decay. It seems that the settlement also slipped into obscurity. Buxton is not even mentioned in the Domesday record of 1086.

By the end of the fifteenth century the 'halywall' or holy well at 'Buckston' (i.e. St Ann's Well) was a celebrated place of pilgrimage, with a reputation for miracles of healing. Despite its closure in 1538 by Sir William Bassett (acting on behalf of Thomas Cromwell, the chief minister of Henry VIII and a prime mover in the Reformation) the well was back in use by 1569, the year after Elizabeth I's accession to the throne, and probably earlier. At that time the Buxton estate belonged to Sir William Cavendish (1505-1557), who had been persuaded to purchase land in Derbyshire by his wife, Bess of Hardwick. In 1572, four years after George Talbot, 6th Earl of Shrewsbury, had become Bess's fourth husband, a Hall was erected over the bath, near the holy well, to provide accommodation for visitors. (The present Old Hall Hotel, built on the site of the Hall, dates from 1670.) While Mary Queen of Scots was in the captivity of the Earl she stayed in the Hall on several occasions, the first being in 1573. Tradition says that in addition to 'taking the waters' for her rheumatism, she explored Poole's Cavern, where a pillar was named after her. When Daniel Defoe visited the Cavern in the early eighteenth century he contemptuously dismissed it as 'another of the wonderless wonders of the Peak'. Adding:

The wit that has been spent upon this vault or cave in the earth, had been well enough to raise the expectation of strangers, and bring fools a great way to creep into it; but is ill bestowed upon all those that come to the place with a just curiosity, founded upon ancient report; when these go in to see it, they generally go away, acknowledging that they have seen nothing suitable to their great expectation, or to the fame of the place.

After being equally dismissive of the 'Queen of Scots Pillar' he concluded: 'in short, there is nothing in Poole's Hole to make a wonder of, any more than as other things in nature, which are rare to be seen, however easily accounted for, may be called wonderful.'

Defoe also visited St Ann's Well, or 'Buxton Bath' as he called it, despite being reluctant to treat the warm spring as a wonder, found himself praising the medicinal virtue of its waters: 'for it is not to be denied, but that wonderful cures have been wrought by them, especially in rheumatic, scorbutic and scrofulous distempers, aches of the joints, nervous pains, and also in scurvy and leprous maladies.'

Given the curative properties of the waters, Defoe suggested that more emphasis should be placed on their use – that, rather than 'wonder at them', people should 'take the benefit of them'. He also anticipated Buxton's development as a spa by recommending that the springs should be: 'built into noble and convenient bathing places; and instead of a house or two, a city built here for the entertainment of company.'

Nevertheless, it was not until the late 1770s that the expansion of Buxton into a fashionable watering place for the wealthy began with a purpose. Using the profits from his copper mines at Ecton in the Manifold Valley, William Cavendish, the 5th Duke of Devonshire, commissioned the York architect, John Carr (1723-1807), to submit plans for the rebuilding and enlargement of the baths. The eventual outcome was The Crescent, built on the foundations of the Roman baths and completed in 1789. It originally contained a variety of accommodation, including a town house for the Duke, shops, an assembly room and an hotel at each end. During its construction, St Ann's Well was demolished and rebuilt near the present Pump Room (built in 1894). By about 1804 the Duke's house, in the centre of the building, had been converted into a third hotel. The Great Stables, also designed by Carr, was built in 1789 to house the horses and carriages of visitors. The large central area, now covered by a huge dome, was used for exercise. In 1859 part of the building was converted into a hospital, with the remainder following in 1878. Its name, 'Devonshire Royal Hospital', honours its ducal benefactors. The houses known as the Square, standing to the west of The Crescent, were designed by John White in 1802-3. The culmination of the 5th Duke's master plan was the construction of the parish church of St John the Baptist, built in the Italianate style, probably by White. Unfortunately, the Duke died in 1811, just before the building was completed.

Despite the development of Lower Buxton around The Crescent, the main centre of settlement in the early nineteenth century lay to the south, at Higher Buxton, where the old village green had become a bustling market place. The narrow street linking one area to the other, was built for the 5th Duke by Carr. St Anne's Church, closed by Sir William Bassett in 1538, was reopened in 1625. Standing near the junction of the main roads from London and Bath, south of the Market Place, it ceased being the parish church in 1812, immediately after its role had been taken over by St John's. Having been used for various purposes, including a school and a mortuary, St Anne's was restored as a place for public worship in 1894. After the death of the 5th Duke (who also built the Eagle on the site of an earlier coaching inn) the Buxton estate passed to his son, William Spencer Cavendish, popularly known as the 'Bachelor Duke'. Although Buxton was then little more than a village, by the time the 6th Duke died in 1858 there could be little doubt that the watering place, with a resident population of around 4,000, had grown, albeit steadily, into a town. Nevertheless, Buxton's greatest expansion occurred after the arrival, in 1863, of two competing railways – the London & North Western and the Midland – who built their stations, one beside the other, above and to the north of The Crescent. Incredibly, a few days after the lines were opened almost 30,000 day trippers arrived by train for the dressing of Buxton's wells.

Unlike his predecessors, who used the Cavendish estates to finance the development of Buxton as a spa, thereby encouraging a sleepy complacency among the inhabitants of the Pennine hollow, the 7th Duke (yet another William Cavendish) pursued a deliberate policy of making the community self-reliant. From his succession in 1858, therefore, Buxton found itself increasingly free to shape its own future. Today, the town may not have succeeded in outshining Bath, as the 5th Duke intended, but its springs are nationally renowned: especially in the profitable form of 'Buxton Natural Mineral Water', which – wonder of wonders – boasts that it is 'bottled at source' from 'The St Ann's Spring'.

SOUTH WING
Little Morton Hall

Considered to be the finest
example of a timber-framed,
moated manor house in Britain,
Little Moreton Hall was built
around a central courtyard by
the Moreton family between
about 1450 and 1580, mainly
using oak from the surrounding
forests. The probable sequence of
construction began with the
Great Hall and the east wing,
followed some thirty years later
by the west wing. The east wing
was subsequently extended south
to include the chapel, and in
1559 the two-storey gabled bay
windows were added to the
Great Hall and Withdrawing
Room (formerly the Old
Parlour). A carved inscription on
the exterior woodwork of the
bay windows states that they
were built by the carpenter
Richard Dale. Another declares
that 'GOD IS AL IN AL
THING'. In addition to the rich
variety of patterns formed by the
timbers, there are a remarkable
variety of shapes in the lead and
glass of the windows. The Long
Gallery, running along the top of
the south wing, was used by
Elizabethans for daily exercise
and games.

RESERVOIR
Goyt's Lane

From Goyt's Lane, a section of
the Cromford & High Peak
Railway dropped down the steep
slope, known as the Bunsall
Incline, before heading north
along the eastern side of the Goyt
Valley to Whaley Bridge. Trains
were hauled up the incline by
means of a stationary steam
engine (fed with water from the
small reservoir in the photograph). Opened in 1831, the
Bunsall Incline was originally
two separate inclines, with a
maximum gradient of 1 in 7: the
upper being 660 yards long with
a vertical rise of 266 feet; and the
lower 455 yards in length with a
rise of 191 feet. They became a
single incline in 1857. Passenger
services ended twenty years later
after a fatal accident. The section
of line between Buxton and
Whaley Bridge, which included
the Goyt Valley, was finally abandoned in 1892. During the construction of the Errwood
Reservoir in the 1960s, the
Bunsall Incline was made into a
road. The plaque at the bottom
of the slope was erected by members of the Stephenson
Locomotive Society in 1972.

'ROCKHALL COTTAGE'
The Roaches

At the southern end of the dramatic gritstone outcrop of the Roaches is a small cottage, built into the base of the rock. Known as 'Rockhall', it was once the home of a gamekeeper. In 1966, thirteen years before the purchase of the Roaches Estate by the Peak National Park, those wanting to climb on the rocks had to pay the 'keeper' a fee of half a crown. 'A notice board indicates these requirements,' wrote W.A. Poucher in *The Peak & Pennines*, 'and climbers are requested to adhere strictly to the paths when walking between the various crags.' Permits to enter the private estate had to be obtained even in the late nineteenth century, as M.J.B. Baddeley noted in *The Peak District* (1899). A ticket of admission was then two old pence. After visiting 'Rock Hall', he wrote: 'The sword of Damocles hung scarce more threatening over the Sicilian tyrant than do the millstone crags over this little rock-fortress.' The cottage is now a memorial hut to Don Whillans (1933-85), the legendary rock-climbing pioneer.

TAXAL EDGE
from Oldgate Nick

The prominent moorland ridge, west of the Goyt Valley, forms the boundary between Derbyshire and Cheshire. From near the Cat and Fiddle public house, it runs northward over Shining Tor, past Oldgate Nick and Pym Chair, to Taxal Edge and Taxal Moor, south-west of Whaley Bridge. The road known as The Street, which descends from Pym Chair to the Goyt Valley, dates back at least to Roman times. Another, more ancient track, once crossed the ridge at Oldgate Nick. Since 1963 large tracts of the high moorland between the county boundary and the Goyt have been planted with conifers by the Forestry Commission, with broadleaved trees like oak, sycamore, beech and sweet chestnut predominating on the lower slopes. As well as supporting sheep and red grouse, the moorland (essentially heather, bilberry, crowberry and coarse grass) is the habitat of hares, rabbits, foxes, voles, skylarks, meadow pipits, wheatears and ring ouzels.

MERMAID'S POOL
Morridge

Tucked secretively below the junction of three, high and exposed moorland roads, a few miles south-east of the Roaches, is a small pool known as Blake Mere, often frozen over in winter. According to legend, it is the haunt of a mermaid, who entices young men to their death by drowning. Some say that the malevolent creature was once human, and that she herself was drowned in the waters after being accused of witchcraft by a rejected suitor. He was later found dead in the pool with deep scratches on his face. On a wall in the nearby public house, known as the Mermaid Inn, is the inscription: 'She calls on you to greet her, combing her dripping crown, and if you go to meet her, she ups and drags you down.' Doxey Pool on the Roaches is also reputed to be the home of a mermaid, or water spirit. The Mermaid's Pool on the western side of Kinder Scout, below Kinder Downfall, is sometimes visited by people in the early morning of Easter Sunday; for it is said that those who see the mermaid will attain immortality.

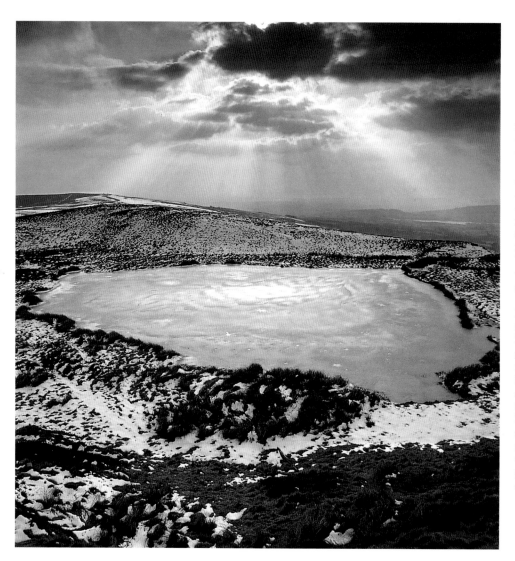

LYME HALL
Lyme Park

Set in a 1,400-acre deer park, some 6 miles south-east of Stockport, Lyme Hall is one of the largest houses in Cheshire. Home of the Legh family since the end of the fourteenth century, the original Elizabethan building (altered in the 1670s) was remodelled and enlarged by the Italian architect, Giacomo Leoni, from about 1725. Further alterations, including the addition of a tower above the portico on the south front, were carried out by Lewis Wyatt in 1814-17. The lead statues crowning the portico represent Venus, Neptune and Pan. In 1688 the five-year-old son of Richard and Elizabeth Legh was tragically drowned in the lake. Richard Legh, 3rd Lord Newton, gave the house and parkland to the National Trust in 1946. The interior decoration, spanning four centuries, includes late seventeenth-century lime wood carving by Grinling Gibbons. Tradition says that if the carved pea-pods (with which Gibbons signed his work) were open he had been paid. The formal gardens are essentially Victorian in style.

JENKIN CHAPEL

Standing in remote isolation at a crossroads on the route of an old salt track across the Cheshire moorland east of Rainow, the church of St John the Baptist, Saltersford, was consecrated on 24 June 1733. Its more familiar name 'Jenkin Chapel' is thought to refer to a packman or drover, who regularly preached at a cross near the site. Another, more fanciful theory, claims that each time a voluntary contribution towards the cost of building the chapel was put in the bag, the collector said 'It's jinkin' '. The tower, with its pitched roof, was added in 1754. At the edge of the road, midway between the chapel and Lamaload Reservoir, is a curious memorial stone. On one side the inscription reads: 'Here John Turner was cast away in a heavy snow storm in the night in or about the year 1755.' The words on the reverse, however, turn what may have been an unfortunate accident into an intriguing mystery: 'The print of a woman's shoe was found by his side in the snow were [sic] he lay dead.'

WARSLOW BROOK VALLEY
near Merryton Low

From its source on the south-eastern side of Merryton Low, the 4-mile-long Warslow Brook rushes past the farming hamlets of Upper and Lower Elkstone before joining the Manifold, below Warslow. (The photograph was taken near the head of the Warslow Brook valley, looking towards Morridge. 'Morridge', or 'moor ridge', stretches for some 10 miles between Flash in the north and Onecote in the south.) The wild, forbidding moorlands hereabouts are a watershed, with streams draining east into the Manifold, south into the Hamps, and west into the Churnet, all of which are tributaries of the Trent. On the 1,603-foot-high hill, Merryton Low, is a triangulation pillar, surmounting a tumulus. The plaque on the side honours the dead of the 5th Staffordshire Leek Battalion Home Guard 'C' Company, killed in action during World War II. The updraughts and thermal currents generated by the steep western escarpment of Morridge is exploited by members of the Staffordshire Gliding Club, whose base is near the Mermaid Inn.

SOLOMON'S TEMPLE
Buxton

Crowning the summit of Grin
Low – the limestone hill overlooking Buxton – the Victorian
folly, known as Solomon's
Temple or Grin Low Tower,
stands on the site of a Neolithic
burial mound. At 1,440 feet
above sea level, the first tower
was erected by Solomon Mycock,
a local farmer, to give work to
Buxton's unemployed. It was
rebuilt in 1896, and is 25 feet
high with an interior spiral staircase leading up to a viewing plat-
form. The Grin Low woodland,
now a Site of Special Scientific
Interest, was planted in 1820 to
cover the unsightly scars of two
hundred years of quarrying and
lime burning. Both the woods
and the temple are now part of
Buxton Country Park. Deep
within the hillside are the underground passages of Poole's
Cavern, one of the so-called
'Wonders of the Peak'. Formed
naturally by the erosive action of
water, the cave takes its name
from a fifteenth-century outlaw,
who is said to have used it as his
den. It is open to the public.

PARISH CHURCH
Leek

Among the many buildings in the
small industrial town of Leek,
associated with William Morris
(1834-96) and the Arts & Crafts
Movement of the late nineteenth
century, are three churches: the
medieval parish church of St
Edward the Confessor, restored
in 1867 by George Edmund
Street (1824-81); the church of St
John the Evangelist, designed by
William Larner Sugden (1850-
1901); and the church of All
Saints, designed by Richard
Norman Shaw (1831-1912).
Among the treasures linked with
Morris in the parish church are
the embroideries undertaken by
the Leek Embroidery Society, led
by Elizabeth Wardle, whose husband, Thomas, owned silk dye-
works in the town. He also col-
laborated with Morris to perfect
vegetable (rather than chemical)
dyeing techniques. Much of the
stained glass in the church was
made by Morris & Co., including
the east window of the north
transept designed by Edward
Burne-Jones. Like St Edwards,
the church of All Saints contains
work by Morris & Co. and the
Leek Embroidery Society.

'FINGER STONE'
Ramshaw Rocks

Located on the Staffordshire moorlands, just east of the Roaches, Ramshaw Rocks possesses several features of interest, including one distinctive gritstone tor that has eroded into a shape resembling a hand with a finger. It points upwards towards the sky (rather than horizontally) because the bedding planes were uplifted and tilted at an angle by movements in the earth's crust over 220 million years ago. Those driving along the Buxton to Leek road, which passes below the jagged wall of stone, may notice the rock formation which looks uncannily like a human face, complete with a hole for the eye. The effect of movement, in relation to the sky and the rocks behind, makes the eye appear to wink. The road, incidentally, was originally built by the Romans. Some of the streams which rise on the moorlands around the Ramshaw Rocks, the Roaches and Hen Cloud feed into the Tittesworth Reservoir, north of Leek, where there is a visitor centre.

SHUTLINGSLOE
near Wildboarclough

Located a few miles south-east of Macclesfield Forest, the peak-like hill of Shutlingsloe (1,659 feet) overlooks the Cheshire Plain to the west and the valley of the Clough Brook to the east. During the disastrous flood of May 1989, a wall of water tore down the Clough Brook Valley, demolishing almost everything in its path: trees were uprooted, bridges washed away and buildings damaged, including some of the cottages at Wildboarclough. It is said that the village takes its name from the tradition that England's last wild boar was killed in the clough. In about 1800 George Palfreyman established a calico-printing factory in the village. Known as Crag Works, it was powered by water from a reservoir on the hillside above. The imposing three-storey administrative wing of the Works (now known as The Old Post Office) is one of the few industrial buildings to survive. The church of St Saviour, consecrated in 1909, was built by the 16th Earl of Derby, who owned the estate.

BUXTON
from Grin Low

Buxton's conversion from a market town into a spa was chiefly
due to the patronage of the
Dukes of Devonshire. After
building The Crescent around a
natural spring in the 1780s, the
5th Duke, William Cavendish,
constructed the Great Stables –
completed in 1789 – to accommodate the horses of visitors to
its hotels. The stables were partly
converted into a hospital in
1859, and in 1881 the large circular courtyard in the centre was
covered by a huge dome, 164
feet in diameter. Known as the
Devonshire Royal Hospital, the
building is prominent in the centre of the photograph. In front of
the hospital can be seen the neo-
classical parish church of St John
the Baptist, built in 1811. The
Opera House, nearby, was
designed by Frank Matcham and
opened in 1903. Since 1979 it
has been the home of the annual
Buxton International Arts
Festival. Immediately next to the
opera house is the Pavilion, built
in 1871. The Palace Hotel
opened in 1868, shortly after the
arrival of two competing railways.

THREE SHIRE HEADS

Five notable rivers rise on the
gritstone moorlands around Axe
Edge, south-west of Buxton: the
Dane and the Goyt flow west to
the Mersey and Irish Sea; while
the Dove, Manifold and Wye
turn east to unite with the Trent
and eventually the North Sea.
Near Flash, the highest village in
England at 1,518 feet above sea
level, the headwaters of the River
Dane are spanned by a small
packhorse bridge, widened at
some time in its history. In
Pannier's Pool, below, the men
and horses rested, washed and
took refreshment. As it stands at
the meeting-point of the three
counties of Cheshire,
Staffordshire and Derbyshire, the
lonely place was not only called
'Three Shire Heads', but it also
became the haunt of roughs and
outlaws, who could readily
escape county justice by crossing
into a different shire. One illegal
enterprise involved the making
and distribution of counterfeit
money. The itinerants, who spent
the winter in Flash, were known
as 'flash-men' and their forged
coins 'flash money'.

FOREST CHAPEL
Macclesfield

Standing in remote and almost
total isolation, high on the hillside above Macclesfield Forest,
the church of St Stephen dates
from 1673, when the first chapel
was built on the site. Before its
construction, the nearest place of
worship for the local farming
community was the parish
church at Macclesfield, some 4
miles distant. The chapel was
entirely rebuilt in 1834, using a
local sandstone known as
Chatsworth Grit. It is thought
that 'S.S.' on the original date
stone (preserved above the doorway in the porch), may stand for
the initials of St Stephen, the first
Christian martyr. The annual
rush-bearing ceremony, held in
the church on the first Sunday
after 12 August, now symbolizes
spiritual renewal. Its origin, however, dates back to the ancient
custom of renewing the rushes
which were strewn on the bare
floors of churches to provide a
warm, dry covering.
Traditionally, the service starts
inside the church, then moves
outside, with the sermon being
delivered by the preacher from
the top of a table tomb.

GOYT BRIDGE

The old packhorse bridge, near
Goytsclough Quarry, originally
stood in the farming hamlet of
Goyt's Bridge, now drowned
beneath the waters of Errwood
Reservoir. In 1965, before the
reservoir was completed, the
bridge was dismantled and reconstructed on its present site, a mile
or so higher up the Goyt Valley.
The nearby gritstone quarry is
noted for being the seventeenth-
century birthplace of Pickfords
Removal Company. Their packhorses used to carry stone slabs
from the quarry to destinations
as far away as London, returning
with goods to be sold in local
towns and villages. The sparse
remains of a nineteenth-century
paint factory and the cottages of
its workers can also be found
near the quarry. Derbyshire
Bridge, even higher up the valley,
was so named because the Goyt
once formed the county boundary between Derbyshire and
Cheshire. In the nineteenth century the area around the Derbyshire
Bridge was mined for coal. Even
Errwood Hall had its own coal
mine.

FERNILEE RESERVOIR

Before the river was dammed to create the Fernilee and Errwood Reservoirs the Goyt Valley farmers were noted for breeding the speckled-faced, hornless Derbyshire Gritstone sheep, originally called the Dale o'Goyt. In addition to sheep, which were hardy enough to survive on the harsh moorland above the valley, they also bred cattle, mainly shorthorns. In *The Derbyshire Dales* (1953) Norman Price described watching 'the dazed Goyt folk' leave the valley in early 1936 to make way for the Fernilee Reservoir. 'The waters bayed up to the sturdy lichened walls of the empty stone farmhouses in the deep of the valley. Then, slowly, the defeated rural men strapped their ancient bedsteads on to hay wagons, fumblingly fastened tin trunks on to their milk carts, and turned away up the lane that led through the deserted village of Fernilee, and all those little windswept streets they would never see again, except as a fading memory.' The remains of a gunpowder factory also lie beneath the waters.

GOYT VALLEY
from Wild Moor

The River Goyt rises on the slopes of Axe Edge Moor, east of the Cat and Fiddle, and flows northwards into the Errwood and Fernilee Reservoirs, through Taxal, Whaley Bridge, New Mills and Marple to enter the River Mersey, near Stockport. The Fernilee Reservoir was completed in 1938, cost almost half a million pounds to build, and has the capacity to hold over 1,000 million gallons. Despite being slightly smaller, with a capacity of 927 million gallons, the Errwood Reservoir cost £1.5 million. It was officially opened on 14 June 1968. Together, the two reservoirs supply the Stockport area with an average of 7-8 million gallons of water a day. In times of drought the remains of farmhouses and cottages are sometimes revealed. Since 1970 the pressure of vast numbers of people visiting the valley has been eased by the strict enforcement of vehicle restrictions. When the central valley is not closed to traffic, a one way system is in operation.

AXE EDGE MOOR
near Dane Head

The gritstone moorland of Axe Edge, rising to a height of over 1,800 feet, gives birth to four rivers: the Dane, the Goyt, the Wye and the Dove. The photograph was taken near the source of the former; while the latter rises from a spring opposite Dove Head Farm on the Leek to Buxton road. The stone covering at Dove Head is carved with a motif made out of the letters C.C. and I.W., representing Charles Cotton and Izaac Walton. In *Gem of the Peak* (1851) William Adam wrote of Axe Edge: 'During the summer of 1842, a party of Royal Sappers and Miners were stationed here, making observations on the surrounding country, and laying down the great lines and most important points for the Government or Ordnance Map. While they were here, parties were stationed on the top of Lincoln Cathedral; a high hill in Nottinghamshire; and also on Snowdon, in Wales, with powerful reflectors, all which points could be distinctly seen in clear weather, although Snowdon is ninety miles distant.'

ERRWOOD HALL

Located on the western side of the Goyt Valley, Errwood Hall was built in 1830 by Samuel Grimshawe, a wealthy Lancastrian industrialist, as a wedding present for his son, Samuel Dominic Grimshawe. The house, with a central tower, and a chapel in the upper storey of the north extension, was purchased by Stockport Corporation Water Undertaking in 1930. After being briefly used as a Youth Hostel, the building was partially demolished to prevent pollution of the planned Fernilee Reservoir. On the hill directly above the ruin is the private cemetery of the Grimshawes. Although the mausoleum has long disappeared, several of the graves remain, including those of S.D. Grimshawe (d. 1883) and John Butler (d. 1886), captain of the family's ocean-going yacht *Mariquita*. The tiny, circular shrine, near the moorland road known as The Street, was erected by the Grimshawes in memory of a Spanish governess. The grounds of Errwood Hall are notable for the many thousands of rhododendrons and azaleas planted by the Grimshawes.

Castleton and the High Peak

After leaving Castleton, the road from Sheffield to Chapel-en-le-Frith passes through the dramatic limestone gorge of Winnats Pass. Local legend maintains that the pass is haunted by the ghosts of an eloping couple, who were murdered there by lead-miners in 1758. Although the killers were never caught, all – except one, who confessed to the crime on his deathbed – met untimely deaths: one hung himself, one went mad, a third was crushed by a rockfall, and another fell off a cliff. Beneath the surface scenery around Castleton is what Conan Doyle described as a hollow country ('The Terror of Blue John Gap'), with vast subterranean caverns formed by the action of water over aeons of time. Several are open to the public, including the Blue John Cavern (a mine containing veins of Blue John, a form of fluorspar) and the Speedwell Cavern (an old lead mine through which visitors can travel by boat on an underground canal). The Treak Cliff Cavern contains some of the finest stalactites in England.

Strategically situated at the southern extremity of the sparsely populated gritstone wilderness of the High Peak, Peveril Castle was built shortly after the Norman Conquest, not only to protect the king's hunting ground – the Royal Forest of the Peak – but to control lead-mining in the area. The fortified village of Castleton, immediately below the castle, was founded towards the end of the twelfth century, probably by Henry II (who, like Henry I, also extended the area of the royal forest). By the beginning of the fourteenth century, the Royal Forest of the Peak covered approximately 180 square miles, and was divided into three wards: Longdendale in the north; Hopedale in the east; and Campagna, the limestone area in the south and west. The boundaries were marked by stone crosses, some of which may still survive, notably at Edale, Hope and Wheston. In extent, the forest stretched west to the River Goyt, north to the Etherow and Longdendale, east to the upper Derwent and south to the upper Wye (which excluded the area south-east of Bradwell Dale and Tideswell). Tideswell, incidentally, was an important administrative centre of the forest and the second largest settlement in Derbyshire during the Middle Ages. Chapel-en-le-Frith, meaning the 'chapel in the forest', grew up around a church founded by the Earl of Derby in 1225. Like Macclesfield Forest, to the west, the hunting rights in the Royal Forest of the Peak were exclusively reserved for the medieval kings. Punishments for those found guilty of infringing the harsh forest laws, particularly in regard to taking deer and game, ranged from fines or imprisonment to the loss of limbs or even death.

The process of clearing the Peak's forest, begun during prehistoric times, continued throughout the Middle Ages and by the seventeenth century the woodland had almost completely disappeared. Natural regeneration of the trees was prevented, for the most part, by great flocks of monastic sheep, which were turned loose on the uplands to graze. By 1536-41, the time of the Dissolution of the Monasteries, the limestone plateau had been transformed into a predominantly agricultural region of ploughland and pasture. Places with 'grange' in the name indicate that they were almost certainly outlying farms belonging to monasteries (some of which, like Dunstable Priory in

Bedfordshire, were far outside the Peak). 'Booth', found in the name of five farming hamlets in Edale, derives from an old Danish word meaning a 'hut or temporary shelter used by herdsmen'.

Although some of the drystone walls in the Peak District are very ancient, the majority of those that exist today date back to the Enclosure Acts of the late eighteenth and early nineteenth centuries, when the large open fields were systematically subdivided into smaller units. At the same time, a number of new farms were created by 'intaking' (the enclosure of areas of waste or uncultivated land, notably on the upper slopes of the moors). One significant outcome of the enclosure movement was a marked increase in dairy farming. In the three-volume *A General View of the Agriculture and Minerals of the County of Derby* (1811-17), John Farey, agent to the Duke of Bedford, noted that 'since enclosure the old limestone sheep have almost entirely given place to dairy cows or to more useful varieties of sheep'.

Today, sheep – including the Peak's two specialist breeds, the Derbyshire Gritstone and the Whitefaced Woodland – can be found throughout the region, even on the highest moors. While cattle (beef as well as dairy) are mainly confined to the lower hills of the limestone plateau. The artificial dewponds, locally known as meres, were constructed to catch rainwater for the animals to drink.

In 1785 two Frenchmen, François and Alexandre La Rochefoucauld, visited Derbyshire and observed that, in addition to producing copper, tin, iron, coal, marble and slate in great abundance, the county had a great variety of landscape: the part that was very hilly contained the mines and the medicinal waters; the remainder, comprising plains and valleys, possessed soil of the greatest fertility and produced an extreme abundance of cattle. On Sunday 27 February, they recorded that the day was one of the coldest they had ever experienced. The road was icy, the wind terrible and the horses slipped so much that they seemed to lose rather than gain ground. After mentioning that they 'crossed some very high peaks and were never on flat ground', the brothers complained about the expensive cost of travelling on the turnpikes – 'which never deserted them in these wild places'. Convinced that the revenue from the roads exceeded the cost of their maintenance, they ended by rebuking the turnpikes for being 'the legalised robbery of all travellers, and a serious robbery at that'.

Almost all of the early writers and travellers who listed the Peak's wonders regarded its hills as wearisome obstacles. Michael Drayton (1563-1631), in *Poly-Olbion*, considered them 'a laborious toil', and likened them to 'a withered beldam' (or hag). Celia Fiennes (1662-1741), who journeyed side-saddle the length and breadth of England, found them 'very steep which makes travelling tedious, and the miles long'. And Daniel Defoe (1660-1731), in *A Tour Thro' the Whole Island of Great Britain*, described them as 'a waste and howling wilderness'. Adding: 'This, perhaps, is the most desolate, wild and abandoned country in all England.'

Yet, like many later writers, Defoe deliberately emphasized the ugliness of the moors so as to heighten, by way of contrast, the beauty of the dales. Here, for example, is how he described his first sight of Chatsworth in the Derwent Valley:

Nothing can be more surprising of its kind, than for a stranger coming from the north, suppose from Sheffield in Yorkshire, ... and wandering or labouring to pass this difficult desert country, and seeing no end of it, and almost discouraged and beaten out with the fatigue of it (just such was our case) on a sudden the guide brings him to this precipice, where he looks down from a frightful height, and a comfortless, barren, and, as he thought, endless moor, into the most delightful valley, with the most pleasant garden, and the most beautiful palace in the world.

In addition to visiting the 'Seven Wonders of the Peak' (which subtly varied from one author to another), nineteenth-century tourists included on their itinerary beauty spots like Dovedale – first made famous by Izaak Walton and Charles Cotton in *The Compleat Angler* (1676). The arrival of the railways during Victorian times opened up the region to the working inhabitants of the surrounding cities, rather than the privileged few.

Nowadays – as a direct result of the pioneering efforts of rock-climbers like James William Puttrell (1869-1939), the culmination of pressure for public access to privately owned tracts of the High Peak (which led to the creation of England's first National Park), and the persistence of long-distance walkers such as Tom Stephenson (1893-1987), who first proposed the Pennine Way – the remote moorlands and gritstone crags are every bit as much enjoyed by visitors, as the gentle limestone hills and dales. Furthermore, below the surface, especially in the area around Castleton, the limestone is riddled with caves, potholes and mine workings. To a lesser extent, these too have become irresistible attractions. Whatever the interest, below as well as above ground, the world of the Peak contains much to be discovered and appreciated.

PEVERIL CASTLE
Castleton

Shortly after the Norman Conquest, William Peverel built Peveril Castle on the summit of a spur of land, protected on all sides by cliffs and steep slopes. Peak Cavern Gorge, on its west side, is 150 feet wide and 230 feet deep. It was formed by the partial collapse of a deep cave system. The huge entrance arch to Peak Cavern, from which passages lead underground to a network of caves, was known as the 'Devil's Arse', and considered to be one of the 'Wonders of the Peak'. It is the largest cave entrance in Britain. So large, in fact, that it once contained the dwellings of local ropemakers. Cave Dale, on the castle's southeast side, was also partly formed by the collapse of a cave roof. In addition to protecting the king's hunting forest, the 'Castle of the Peak' also played an important role in guarding the lead mines of the area. The keep, the highest point of the castle, was built by Henry II in 1176-77. Today the ruins are in the care of English Heritage.

MARKET PLACE
Castleton

The medieval village of Castleton – with its church at the centre and market place to the south – was laid out on a grid plan towards the end of the twelfth century. Although the settlement, immediately below Peveril Castle, was originally protected by a defensive bank and ditch, only traces of the earthwork now remain. The Norman church of St Edmund, standing on a low mound, was largely rebuilt in the nineteenth century. Its finest feature is undoubtedly the Norman arch between the nave and chancel. The cross in the market place is a war memorial. Close by, several plaques list the names of local men who lost their lives during World War I. Each year, on 'Garland Day' (29 May), the village holds a unique ceremony that was originally an ancient fertility rite. Suppressed by Cromwell, it was revived to celebrate Charles II's restoration to the throne in 1660. The 'King', encased from head to waist in a bell-shaped garland of flowers, rides through the streets with his 'Consort' to scenes of much merriment.

ODIN MINE
near Castleton

Reputedly named after the Norse god of war, the Odin Mine – just over a mile north-west of Castleton – is one of the oldest and best known lead mines in Derbyshire. After being brought to the surface, the lead ore was shovelled onto a horizontal cast iron ring and crushed by a heavy gritstone wheel, hauled round by a horse. The iron tyre around the wheel was held in place with wooden wedges. Prior to smelting, the crushed ore was washed to separate the heavy lead from the lighter spoil. The waste, piled into heaps, can still be seen close by. William Adam in *Gem of the Peak* (1851) said that the ore also yielded about three ounces of silver per ton. (The photograph was taken looking across the crushing circle, erected in 1823, to Hollins Cross and Back Tor.) Like most abandoned mine workings, the Odin Mine is highly dangerous and should not be entered. It is one of very few mines in the Peak District with an entrance big enough to accommodate a horse and cart, hence the name 'Cartgate'.

HIGH PEAK
from Higger Tor

The moors of the Peak District reach their highest elevation north of Mam Tor and Castleton. Although known as the High Peak, they also form the bulk of the Dark Peak, of which the underlying rock is millstone grit. In contrast to the softer, limestone country of the White Peak, the gritstone landscape is essentially peat and heather moorland and, therefore, far less populated. The few villages and farmsteads that can be found tend to shelter in the river valleys, and be smaller, more isolated, and more self-sufficient that those further south. Scattered throughout this bleak and desolate wilderness are the rusting remains of countless aircraft that have tragically crashed while flying across the High Peak. In two books on *Dark Peak Aircraft Wrecks,* Ron Collier, an ex-Royal Air Force pilot, lists many of the crash sites, as well as relating the stories of almost sixty flying accidents, involving aircraft ranging in type from biplanes to military jet fighters. Miraculously, some of those involved managed to survive.

MAM TOR
near Castleton

On the grassy, 1,695-foot summit
of Mam Tor – dominating the
head of the Hope Valley two
miles north-west of Castleton –
are the earthwork remains of an
Iron Age hillfort. Covering 16
acres, it stands on the site of a
Bronze Age settlement dating
back to over 1000 BC, and is the
largest hillfort in the Peak
District. Known to the Celts as
the 'Mother Mountain', Mam
Tor is connected to the 1,563-
foot Lose Hill by an ancient
track which runs along the crest
of a sandstone and shale ridge.
Because of the instability of the
sedimentary rocks, the slopes of
Mam Tor are constantly crumbling (hence its popular name of
'Shivering Mountain'). At some
time in the past a large section of
the hill slipped away leaving the
sheer, exposed face shown in the
photograph. In 1979, two years
after a dramatic landslip, the
Mam Tor section of the old
A625 trans-Pennine road was
permanently closed to through
traffic. The bypass winds steeply
through Winnats Pass.

KINDER VALLEY
from Kinder Scout

From its source on the peat-
covered moorland plateau of
Kinder Scout, the River Kinder
flows over the rocky cleft of
Kinder Downfall and into the
valley below to feed the Kinder
Reservoir (in the centre of the
photograph). During dry weather
the waterfall is often reduced to a
trickle and may even dry up completely. On occasions, when the
wind is in the right direction, the
water is blown back up the face
of the 100-foot Downfall to create a huge fountain of spray.
Long ago, the Downfall was
known as Kinder Scut ('scut'
meaning a projecting cliff or
overhanging rock). Today, however, 'Kinder Scout' is taken to
refer to the plateau. While
'Kinder' embraces the whole of
the surrounding moorland massif.
The highest point of Kinder
Scout, which lacks a clearly
defined summit, is 2,088 feet
above sea level. It is also the
highest point in the Peak. In fact,
the Peak District is not a land of
peaks. The name 'peak' derives
from the Old English word for
hill, any kind of hill.

KINDER RESERVOIR

Completed in 1911, the Kinder Reservoir – with its distinctive filter house – was built in the upper Kinder Valley, above Hayfield, to supply water to the Stockport area. (Hayfield, after protests, managed to retain its own water supply at Harrymoor.) Construction materials, including local stone and clay, were carried up to the Kinder Reservoir site by a small railway, which ran from Hayfield Station to the dam. Today, little trace of the 2-mile line remains. Likewise, the dam workers' shanty or 'Tin Town', erected on the banks of the Kinder, north of Bowden Bridge, has also disappeared. It was from Bowden Bridge Quarry that the celebrated 'Mass Trespass' onto Kinder Scout started on Sunday 24 April 1932. The historic event is commemorated at the quarry by a bronze plaque, unveiled in 1990 by Benny Rothman, one of the five so-called ringleaders who were imprisoned for the action. Their severe sentences proved to be a major catalyst in the campaign for access to the private moorland.

LADYBOWER RESERVOIR

The reservoirs of Howden and Derwent were constructed in the Upper Derwent Valley before World War I to provide water for the expanding industrial towns of Sheffield, Derby, Nottingham and Leicester. The supply, however, proved to be inadequate and a third dam was built some 3 miles further down the valley, creating the Ladybower Reservoir. Construction took place between 1935 and 1943. After completion, the valley to the north was flooded, and in the process the Derbyshire villages of Derwent and Ashopton were submerged. Although most of the buildings of Derwent village were demolished and the stone used to strengthen the reservoir, the packhorse bridge was dismantled stone by stone and reconstructed at Slippery Stones, above the head of Howden Reservoir. Sometimes, when the waters are abnormally low, the ruins of Derwent reappear. The remains of Ashopton – an important coaching-stop on the 1821 turnpike road between Sheffield and Glossop – lie so deep underwater that they may never be seen again.

WESTEND MOSS
from Wilmer Hill

When the wind stops howling
and the rain stops pouring, the
distinctive sounds of the moorland's hidden wildlife are often
revealed, according to season: the
haunting, melancholy call of the
curlew; the explosive, whirring
flight of the red grouse; the rat-
tling chatter of the ring ouzel or
mountain blackbird; the echoing,
flutey song of the golden plover
(so-called 'watchman of the
moors'); and the conspicuous
series of liquid notes uttered in
flight by the meadow pipit,
which gradually increase in
tempo to end with a congratula-
tory trill. Those with sensitive
ears may hear the movements of
more furtive creatures among the
dwarf shrubs and rough grasses:
the rustle of the adder or viper,
Britain's only poisonous snake;
and the scraping of the mountain
or blue hare, the coat of which
turns wholly or partially white in
winter. Re-introduced on the
moors of the Peak in the nineteenth century, these small, rab-
bit-sized animals feed mainly on
heather, and mostly at night.

PARISH CHURCH
Hayfield

Standing on the River Sett, which
merges with the Kinder at
Bowden Bridge, Hayfield was
recorded in the Domesday survey
of 1086 and dates back at least
to Anglo-Saxon times. Originally,
the settlement developed at the
meeting-point of several routes. It
not only stands on the old
Roman road between Melandra
Castle fort (near Glossop) and
Aquae Arnemetiae (Buxton), but
during medieval times it was an
important trading centre on several packhorse routes – the
busiest carrying dyed and woven
woollen goods to Glossop and
Holmfirth, beyond. The church
of St Matthew, overlooking the
weir and Memorial Garden, was
rebuilt on the site of a medieval
foundation in 1818, while the
tower was added in 1894. The
Garden commemorates three
young people killed in a tragic
accident during the Hayfield Jazz
Festival of 1983. Over the centuries the village has suffered
serious flood damage. The worst
in 1748 tore through the churchyard, causing the dead to be
swept from their graves.

BLACKDEN BARN
Ashop Valley

The creation of turnpike toll
roads in the seventeenth and
eighteenth centuries led to a
great improvement in the stan-
dards of highways and, conse-
quently, an increase in trade.
Although the turnpike system
was basically unpopular, at its
peak there were around 30,000
miles of turnpikes criss-crossing
Britain. However, by the end of
the nineteenth century, as a direct
result of the introduction of railways, the system had completely
collapsed. One reminder of the
turnpike era in the Peak District
is the Snake Road, engineered by
Thomas Telford (1757-1834) and
completed in 1821. Bypassing the
original Sheffield to Manchester
turnpike, which went through
Hathersage and Castleton,
Telford's new route headed
north-west up the Ashop Valley
and over the 1,680-foot-high
Snake Pass to Glossop. The village of Ashopton (now submerged by the Ladybower
Reservoir) grew up around the
Cocksbridge toll-bar. Blackden
Barn is part of the National
Trust's High Peak Estate.

BLACK ASHOP MOOR

Among the legends of the Peak
District are stories of ghostly
black dogs, with large saucer-
shaped eyes, which haunt desolate moorland roads, often at
night or in mist. In some areas
their appearance, especially at a
crossroads, was considered to be
an omen of death. More often
than not, however, the phantom
creature appears from nowhere,
follows the traveller along the
road, and then disappears as suddenly as it came. Sometimes people have the sensation of being
followed by a large animal, but
on turning round are unable to
see or hear anything. Although
the dogs have been encountered
at various isolated spots, including bridges, their presence on
moors is mainly attributed to
guarding graves or murder sites.
Nevertheless, one person they did
not seem to bother was Thomas
Bateman (1821-61), the indefati-
gable antiquarian who excavated
over 400 prehistoric burial
mounds in the Peak. His railed
tomb stands in a field behind the
former Congregational Chapel at
Middleton-by-Youlgreave.

DERWENT DAM

Described by Defoe as 'a fright-ful creature when the hills load her current with water', the Derwent is the principal river of the Peak District. Rising on the wild, uninhabited moorland of Bleaklow, it flows in a south-eastern direction – past Hathersage, Chatsworth, Matlock, Belper and Derby – to join the Trent near Shardlow. Much of the upper Derwent Valley has been flooded to create the Howden, Derwent and Ladybower Reservoirs, simply known as 'the Dams'. Being the largest of over fifty reservoirs in the National Park, they have been dubbed the Peak's Lake District. The workers who built both the Howden and Derwent Dams lived in the temporary set-tlement of Birchinlee. Long dis-mantled, their 'Tin Town' stood on the west bank of the valley between the two construction sites. A memorial on the Derwent Dam commemorates the Dambusters, 'who successfully breached the dams of Western Germany in World War II using the bouncing bomb devised by Dr Barnes Wallis'.

PARISH CHURCH
Holmbridge

The church of St David's at Holmbridge was designed by R.D. Chantrell and erected in 1838-40. The chancel was added in 1887. Although built by the Church of England, the building is now shared by local Methodists as well as Anglicans. In 1944 a sudden cloudburst over Holme Moss caused a flash-flood to sweep down the valley leaving a trail of destruction. The worst flood disaster, however, was caused by the bursting of the Bilberry Dam, above Holmbridge, in 1852. Completed in 1842, the Bilberry Reservoir was linked exactly 110 years later to the larger Digley Reservoir. Water from both reser-voirs (together with water from the Brownhill Reservoir complex) is purified at the treatment works near Holmbridge. From there it is piped to the area around Huddersfield, Batley and Halifax. A gravestone in the churchyard at Holmbridge commemorates eleven workmen killed during the construction of the Yateholme and Riding Wood Reservoirs in 1872-76. One was a twelve-year-old boy.

ASHOPTON VIADUCT

The A57 Sheffield to Glossop road is carried across the Ladybower Reservoir by the steel-and-concrete Ashopton Viaduct, constructed in the early 1940s. Its massive arches stand on the ruins of Ashopton village, 100 feet under the water. The reservoir, officially opened by King George VI on 25 September 1945, has a storage capacity of 6,300 million gallons. While the daily quantity of water available from the three linked reservoirs (Howden, Derwent and Ladybower) is approximately 50 million gallons. Surplus water in the Ladybower Reservoir escapes through two 15-foot-diameter, funnel-shaped overflows, situated near the dam. Locally, they are known as 'the plug holes'. In order to ensure an adequate flow of water in the Derwent below the reservoirs, around 17 million gallons a day is released into the river. The rest is piped to the water treatment works at Bamford, 2 miles to the south. Ladybower is also used as a still-water trout fishery.

HINCHLIFFE MILL

The woollen-weaving village of Hinchliffe Mill, in the Holme Valley, sprang up in the late eighteenth century around a manorial corn mill owned by the Earnshaws of Holme. 'Hinchliffe' is thought to have been the name of the miller. Most of the houses, which rise up the steep hillside, were built with three storeys to accommodate the weavers' looms on the upper floor. The industrial expansion, brought about by water-driven and then steam-powered woollen mills, also led to the rapid and haphazard development of Holmfirth into a textile-manufacturing town. Today, in addition to its television connection with *Last of the Summer Wine*, Holmfirth is also associated with the firm of Bamforths, one of the early pioneers of motion pictures. Founded by James Bamford in 1870, the company progressed from producing magic lantern slides, through picture postcards, to silent movies. Their work, including saucy seaside postcards, can be seen in the Holmfirth Postcard Museum

NOE STOOL
Kinder

Noe Stool, one of Kinder's much-photographed landmarks, takes its name from the Vale of Edale's main river, which rises nearby. Also known as the Anvil, the outcrop is one of a series of grit-stone tors in the High Peak to have been sculpted by the elements into a fascinating variety of formations. Like the cluster of rock shapes that litter the southern edge of the Kinder Scout plateau, Noe Stool is a defiant remnant of what was once a much larger gritstone mass. Gritstone, in fact, is a coarse-grained sandstone and was laid down on top of the limestone in alternation with other sedimentary materials, including shales. The latter rocks, which are prone to landslips, predominate in the sandstone-shale ridge – running from Mam Tor to Lose Hill – on the opposite side of the Edale valley. The distinctive escarpment south-west of Noe Stool (and shown in the photograph) is Swine's Back: so-named because when viewed from certain angles it resembles the back of a pig.

FIELD BARN
Upper Booth

From the Old Nag's Head in the village of Edale there are two official Pennine Way routes up onto Kinder Scout. Both unite at Kinder Downfall to continue north as a single path. The main route climbs north-west up Grindsbrook Clough and over the peat-covered plateau. While the alternative bad-weather route heads west along the Edale valley to Upper Booth, from where (passing the barn in the photograph) it attains the summit of Kinder Low by way of Jacob's Ladder. The 270-mile Pennine Way, stretching from Edale along the backbone of England to the Scottish village of Kirk Yetholm in the Borders, was officially opened in 1965. Yet the idea of a route along the Pennines was first proposed in 1935 by the journalist Tom Stephenson (1893-1987) in a *Daily Herald* article. His original notion was to call the route the Jubilee Trail, in commemoration of George V's Silver Jubilee. Sadly, the popularity of the Pennine Way has caused serious erosion problems, especially on peat moors like Kinder.

MOAT STONE
Kinder

Situated on the edge of the
Kinder Scout plateau between
Noe Stool and Crowden Tower
are a series of gritstone tors
called the Woolpacks (also
known as the Mushroom Garden
or Whipsnade). Among the many
rock formations in the area is the
isolated block, popularly referred
to as the Moat Stone because it
is normally completely encircled
by water. (When this photograph
was taken, however, the surface
of the notoriously soggy peat
moorland on the plateau was
unnaturally dry.) Over the years
several aircraft have crashed in
the locality, including a Harvard
FT415 of the Fleet Air Arm
which disappeared on 14 January
1952 during a routine training
flight. Although the pilot had
officially set off from
Nottinghamshire to fly south to
Kemble in the Cotswolds, just
over 100 miles away, his dead
body was discovered – still seat-
ed in the cockpit of his crashed
plane – near the Woolpacks,
some 50 miles off course. Why
he had flown in completely the
wrong direction remains a mystery.

THE WOOLPACKS
Kinder

The gritstone outcrops known as
the Woolpacks, on the southern
edge of the Kinder Scout plateau
overlooking Edale, can be
reached on foot by several routes
– the easiest is probably by way
of Upper Booth, Jacob's Ladder,
Swine's Back and Noe Stool. In
the past the blanket of peat on
the moorland was covered by
dwarf shrubs like heather and
bilberry, but overgrazing by
sheep in the twentieth century
has led to the rapid spread of
rough grasslands. It has been estimated that 30 percent of heather
in the Peak District was lost after
the introduction of government
subsidies in the 1940s, which
encouraged farmers to keep more
sheep on the moors than the vegetation could sustain. Nowadays,
heather and bilberry are mainly
found at the edge of the plateau.
In addition to changes in farming
practices, other factors like
atmospheric pollution and acci-
dental fires have contributed to
the creation of the present moorland landscape

EDALE HEAD
from Rushup Edge

Watered by the River Noe, which joins the Derwent near Bamford, the valley of Edale contains a string of five farming hamlets known as 'booths' – Upper Booth, Barber Booth, Grindsbrook Booth, Ollerbrook Booth and Nether Booth. A 'Booth' or 'bothie' was a hut or temporary shelter used by herdsmen. Most of the Edale settlements lie on the northern side of the valley and are, therefore, best positioned to catch as much of the sparse winter sunshine as possible. After the arrival of the Sheffield to Manchester railway line in 1894, the communities in Edale ceased to be remote and isolated. Construction of the 2-mile-long Cowburn tunnel under Colborne Moor, at the head of the valley, began in 1888. It is one of the deepest in England. Jacob's Ladder, near the ruins of Edale Head House, was named after Jacob Marshall, a 'jagger' or packhorse train leader, who made the original steps in the eighteenth century. Edale Cross, to the west, was a boundary marker of the Royal Forest of the Peak.

HOLME AND UPPERTHONG

Standing in the pencil-thin shadow of the Holme Moss television transmitter mast, the hilltop village of Holme overlooks Holmbridge and the Holme Valley. From its source near the mast, the River Holme flows north-west into the Brownhill Reservoir before continuing its 9-mile journey – through Holmbridge, Hinchliffe Mill and Holmfirth – to join the River Colne at Huddersfield. Above the valley are several villages built of local Yorkshire sandstone or millstone grit: Upperthong, Netherthong, Honley, Wooldale and Hepworth. All, to a greater or lesser degree, were involved in the woollen textile industry which dominated the valley in the nineteenth century. This is evident in the two- and three-storey weavers' cottages (with a long row of mullioned windows on the upper floors to give more light to the looms). Probably the most unusual dwelling in the area is 'Underhill' at Holme, an 'underground' house built by the architect Arthur Quarmby.

YEOMAN HEY RESERVOIR

In order to meet the demand for clean, unlimited water, especially from the thirsty cities and towns that ring the Peak National Park, numerous reservoirs have been created on the gritstone uplands by damming rivers and streams. The Yeoman Hey Reservoir on Saddleworth Moor is one of a series of four which occupy the linked valleys of the Greenfield and Chew Brooks (the others being the Greenfield, Dovestone and Chew Reservoirs). Like most reservoirs in the Peak, they also exploit the fact that the Pennines attract far more than the average amount of rainfall. Whereas in the past the public were banned from the private land around the reservoirs, the various water authorities now actively encourage access. In addition to providing car parks and picnic sites, improving existing paths and creating new routes, they have also attempted to make these artificial, water-filled valleys attractive, both to visitors and to wildlife.

THE TOWER
Alport Castles

Despite looking like the crumbling ruins of an artificial fortress, the Tower at Alport Castles – 2 miles west of Derwent Reservoir – is an entirely natural formation. It is, in fact, an isolated mass of eroded gritstone and shale that has slowly detached itself from the main cliff of Alport Castles, one of the largest and most spectacular landslips in Britain. Lying in the shadow of the shifting landscape of cliffs, chasms and boulders is Alport Castles Farm (seen in the photograph). At the end of the seventeenth century, when unauthorized religious meetings were banned, the modest gritstone barn at the remote farmstead became a place of refuge for persecuted non-conformists. John Wesley (1703-91), founder of the Methodist Movement, is reputed to have preached there several times. Today, an annual sacramental ceremony, known as the 'Woodlands Lovefeast', is held in the barn on the first Sunday in July. A 'lovefeast' is a 'Feast of Charity' in which the rich feed the poor.

HOLME VALLEY
from White Gate

During medieval times the two main industries in the Holme Valley area were sheep farming and woollen-cloth manufacture, the latter being carried out in the homes of the weavers. The plentiful supplies of soft water coming down from the surrounding gritstone moors proved ideal for the washing and fulling processes. Although hand looms continued to be used until well into the nineteenth century, the invention of Kay's flying shuttle in 1733, Hargreaves' Spinning Jenny in c.1764 and Cartwright's power loom in 1785 inevitably led to the mechanization of the cloth-making process, and the rapid expansion of the industry. Instead of driving corn mills, the fast-flowing river found itself powering an increasing number of woollen mills. The shift from hand looms in the home to power looms in the factory brought about the factory system and the exploitation of cheap child labour. It is reported that the Holme Valley flood of 1852 put 4,898 adults and 2,142 children out of work.

BLEAKLOW
from Alport Low

The 3-mile section of the Pennine Way from the Snake Road across Alport Low to Bleaklow Head (2,060 feet above sea level) was once considered to be the toughest part of the long-distance walk. In his classic *Pennine Way Companion* (1968), Alfred Wainwright agreed that 'it is certainly mucky, too often belaboured by rain and wind, and weird and frightening in mist'. Yet, with characteristic humour, he offered the following advice: 'cheer up. There is worse to follow.' About half a mile north of the Snake Road, the Way crosses an old Roman road which ran from Navio (Brough) to Melandra Castle fort (near Glossop). This track, known as Doctor's Gate, is thought to have been named after a doctor from Glossop, who regularly travelled along the route in the sixteenth century. The name itself was first recorded in 1627. In this bleak and desolate area the terrain can be confusing – eroded peat groughs, boggy hollows and grassy hummocks, with only a few isolated boundary posts to help identify the way.

WILLIAM CLOUGH
near Ashop Head

William Clough – the steep rocky valley which runs from the summit of the Kinder plateau to the Kinder Reservoir – is reputedly named after a miner (or blacksmith), who had a smelting works (or smithy) in the vicinity. From Hayfield, a 6-mile footpath known as the Snake Path climbs up the clough onto Ashop Head to end at the Snake Pass Inn in the Ashop Valley. The inn, despite being 1,086 feet above sea level is over 600 feet lower than the Cat and Fiddle (on Goyt's Moss, west of Buxton) which has the distinction of being the second highest pub in England. A Victorian view of Kinder Scout from near the Snake Pass Inn, with a lone fisherman sitting on the banks of the River Ashop, was painted in 1879 by George Turner (1843-1910), the so-called 'Derbyshire Constable'. His gravestone, which had been lost for many years, was rediscovered in 1992 in a corner of the churchyard at Idridgehay. The Pennine Way long distance footpath crosses the Snake Path near Ashop Head and the summit of William Clough.

HOLMFIRTH

Straddling the River Holme, just outside the northern boundary of the Peak National Park, the Pennine textile town of Holmfirth is noted for being the centre of 'Summer Wine Country' – the area in West Yorkshire where the BBC set their long-running television comedy series *Last of the Summer Wine*, starring such endearing characters as Compo, Clegg and the wrinkled-stockinged Nora Batty. The Georgian church of the Holy Trinity, which often appears in the scenes, was built to replace the previous foundation which was severely damaged in the flood of 1777. A brass plaque on the nearby monument, known as 'T'owd Genn' (possibly after Henry Genn a seventeenth-century stonemason), commemorates the terrible flood of 5 February 1852, when the Bilberry Reservoir burst its banks and eighty-one people lost their lives. The height reached by the floodwater is marked on the monument, erected in 1801 to mark the 'Peace of Amiens', the fourteen-month interlude in Britain's war with France.

PHOTOGRAPHER'S NOTES

The valley of the River Noe – between the Kinder escarpments and the Great Ridge (which includes Lord's Seat, Mam Tor, Hollins Cross and Lose Hill) – has anciently been known as Edale. But, after the arrival of the railway in 1894, the name 'Edale' was also applied to the gritstone village of Grindsbrook Booth. Before the consecration of the village's first church and graveyard in 1633, the bodies of the deceased had to be carried to Castleton over Hollins Cross for burial. The present church, dedicated to the Holy and Undivided Trinity, was started in 1885 and consecrated by the Bishop of Southwell in 1886. The tower and spire were completed a few years later. In fact, it is the village's third church, and stands across the road from the old graveyard where the two previous foundations were sited. As well as the Old Nag's Head and the Rambler Inn, the village contains a National Park Information Centre, a Mountain Rescue Post and a railway station.

I have come to the conclusion that landscape photography is not only tough on boots, it is tough on cameras. In fact, it's tough on all the equipment that I use. For, over the years, I've had to replace more than I would have liked: tripods eventually seize; filters obviously become scratched; cable-releases snap ... the list is endless.

Essentially, I use two types of cameras: one takes 35mm film (the size most commonly used for general photographs – buildings, villages, wildlife and so on); the other takes the larger 120 film (primarily used for landscapes). Experience has shown that they fall into two categories – the sublime and the ridiculous. My Nikon F3 belongs to the former. It is the only 35mm camera I've ever used professionally, is years old, has had thousands of films put through it, and has been accidentally dropped several times, has continued to work through all kinds of weather conditions from baking heat to freezing cold, yet it has never gone wrong. In fact, it has been faultless. One day it may be retired to the mantelpiece, but I very much doubt that I shall ever part with it. The larger format of camera, however, belongs to the latter category. Despite trying various different makes, I have not yet found one that is totally reliable.

The pictures I take depend heavily upon suitable weather conditions. When it is dull I research locations. When the light is good I try to be on the spot with the camera clicking. Often I walk miles to seek out a suitable viewpoint. If the light is not right for photography, I make various notes (including taking compass readings and visualizing the weather conditions that will best fit the scene). All this is carried out with the intention of returning on some future occasion when the weather is more befitting to the landscape. Working in this way is not only time-consuming, it can be extremely frustrating. But when the designated scene is illuminated in reality, just as it had been visualized in imagination, and the camera shutter is clicking furiously, the rewards are very special indeed. Until, yet again, the larger-format camera lets me down. The search continues and the soles wear thin.

Rob Talbot

SELECTED PROPERTIES
AND REGIONAL OFFICES

PEAK NATIONAL PARK

National Park Office
Aldern House
Baslow Road
Bakewell
Derbyshire DE45 1AE
Tel: (01629) 816200

National Park Study Centre
Losehill Hall
Peak National Park Centre
Castleton
Derbyshire S30 2WB
Tel: (01433) 620373

ENGLISH HERITAGE

Head Office
23 Savile Row
London W1X 1AB
Tel: (0171) 973 3000

Historic Properties Midlands & East Anglia
Hazelrigg House
33 Marefair
Northampton NN1 1SR
Tel: (01604) 730320

Arbor Low Stone Circle
c/o Peak Park Joint Planning Board
Aldern House
Baslow Road
Bakewell
Derbyshire DE45 1AE
Tel: (01629) 816200
Open any reasonable time throughout year.

Hardwick Old Hall
Doe Lea
near Chesterfield
Derbyshire DE24 2DJ
Tel: (01246) 850431
Open April to October, Wednesdays to Sundays.

Peveril Castle
Market Place
Castleton
Derbyshire S30 2WX
Tel: (01433) 620613
Open daily April to October; November to March, Wednesdays to Sundays.

Wingfield Manor
Manor Road
South Wingfield
near Alfreton
Derbyshire DE5 7NH
Tel: (01773) 832060 (Information line)
Open April to October, Wednesdays to Sundays and Bank Holiday Mondays; November to March, Wednesdays to Sundays.

NATIONAL TRUST

N.T. Regional Visitors' Guides are usually available from Tourist Information Centres in 'home' regions.

East Midlands Regional Office
Clumber Park Stableyard
Worksop
Nottinghamshire S80 3BE
Tel: (01909) 486411

Mercia Regional Office
Attingham Park
Shrewsbury
Shropshire SY4 4TP
Tel: (01743) 709343

Biddulph Grange Garden
Biddulph Grange
Biddulph
Stoke-on-Trent
Staffordshire ST8 7SD
Tel: (01782) 517999
Open April to end October, Wednesdays to Sundays and Bank Holiday Mondays; closed Good Friday; November to December, weekends only.

Hardwick Hall
Doe Lea
Chesterfield
Derbyshire S44 5QJ
Tel: (01246) 850430
House open end March to early November, Wednesdays, Thursdays, Saturdays, Sundays and Bank Holiday Mondays; garden open daily April to early November.

Ilam Park
Ilam
Ashbourne
Staffordshire DE6 2AZ
Tel: (01335) 350245
Grounds and park open daily throughout year. Hall is let to YHA and is not open.

Kedleston Hall
Derby
Derbyshire DE22 5JH
Tel: (01332) 842191
House and garden open end March to early November, Saturdays to Wednesdays; park open daily throughout year.

Little Moreton Hall
Congleton
Cheshire CW12 4SD
Tel: (01260) 272018
Open end March to end October, Wednesdays to Sundays and Bank Holiday Mondays; November to mid-December, weekends only.

Longshaw Estate
Sheffield
Derbyshire S11 7TZ
Tel: (01433) 631708 (Visitor Centre)
Tel: (01433) 631757 (Warden's Office)
Visitor Centre open weekends throughout year and Bank Holiday Mondays; also Wednesdays and Thursdays from end March to December; estate open daily throughout year.

Lyme Park
Disley
Stockport
Cheshire SK12 2NX
Tel: (01663) 762023 (766492 for information)
*House open Easter to end October,
Saturdays to Wednesdays; Garden open
April to end October daily; November to
end March (ring for details); park open
daily throughout year.*

Sudbury Hall
Sudbury
Ashbourne
Derbyshire DE6 5HT
Tel: (01283) 585305
*House and grounds open end March to
early November, Wednesdays to Sundays
and Bank Holiday Mondays; closed Good
Friday.*

**Sudbury: The National Trust Museum
of Childhood**
Sudbury
Ashbourne
Derbyshire DE6 5HT
Tel: (01283) 585305
*Open end March to early November,
Wednesdays to Sundays and Bank Holiday
Mondays; closed Good Friday.*

MISCELLANEOUS

Alton Towers
Alton
Staffordshire ST10 4DB
Tel: (0990) 204060 (enquiries)
*Leisure Park open March to early
November; gardens open daily
throughout year.*

Blue John Cavern
Castleton
Derbyshire S30 2WP
Tel: (01433) 620638/620642
*Open daily throughout year (weather
permitting), except Christmas.*

Chatsworth House
Chatsworth
Bakewell
Derbyshire DE45 1PP
Tel: (01246) 582204
*House and garden open daily end March
to end October; farmyard & adventure
playground open daily end March to
early October.*

Cromford Mill
Mill Lane
Cromford
Matlock
Derbyshire DE4 3RQ
Tel: (01629) 824297
*Open daily throughout year, except
Christmas Day.*

Eyam Hall
Eyam
Derbyshire S30 1QW
Tel: (01433) 631976
*Open April to end October, Wednesdays,
Thursdays, Sundays and Bank Holidays,
Mondays and Tuesdays.*

Haddon Hall
The Estate Office
Bakewell
Derbyshire DE45 1LA
Tel: (01629) 812855
*House and Gardens open daily from April
to end September; closed Sundays in July
and August.*

Peak Cavern
Peak Cavern House
Castleton
Derbyshire S30 2WS
Tel: (01433) 620285
Open daily Easter to end October.

Peak District Mining Museum
The Pavilion
Matlock Bath
Derbyshire DE4 3NR
Tel: (01629) 583834
*Open daily throughout year, except
Christmas Day.*

Poole's Cavern
Green Lane
Buxton
Derbyshire SK17 9DH
Tel: (01298) 26978
Open daily March to end October.

Riber Castle Wildlife Park
Riber Castle
Matlock
Derbyshire DE4 5JU
Tel: (01629) 582073
*Open daily throughout year, except
Christmas Day.*

Speedwell Cavern
Winnat's Pass
Castleton
Derbyshire S30 2WA
Tel: (01433) 620512
*Open daily throughout year, except
Christmas.*

Temple Mine
Temple Road
Matlock Bath
Derbyshire DE4 3PS
Tel: (01629) 583834
*Open daily throughout year, except
Christmas Day.*

Treak Cliff Cavern
Castleton
Derbyshire S30 2WP
Tel: (01433) 620571
*Open daily throughout year, except
Christmas Day.*

SELECT BIBLIOGRAPHY

Adam, William, *Gem of the Peak*, Moorland Publishing, Buxton, 1973 (1st pub. 1851)
Baddeley, M.J.B., *The Peak District* (Thorough Guide series), Dulau, London, 1899
Bellamy, Rex, *The Peak District Companion*, David & Charles, Newton Abbot, 1981
The Cheshire Village Book, Countryside Books, Newbury, 1990
Christian, Roy, *The Peak District*, David & Charles, Newton Abbot, 1976
Clarke, David, *Ghosts and Legends of the Peak District*, Jarrold, Norwich, 1991
Collier, Ron, *Dark Peak Aircraft Wrecks 2*, Leo Cooper, London, 1992 (1st pub. 1982)
Collier, Ron, and Wilkinson, Roni, *Dark Peak Aircraft Wrecks 1*, Leo Cooper, London, 1990 (1st pub. 1979)
Daniel, Clarence, *The Story of Eyam Plague*, Country Bookstore Publications, Bakewell, 1977
Defoe, Daniel, *A Tour Thro' the Whole Island of Great Britain*, Davies, London, 1927 (1st pub. 1724-6)
The Derbyshire Guide, Derbyshire Countryside, Derby, 1971
The Derbyshire Village Book, Countryside Books, Newbury, 1991
Devonshire, The Duchess of, *The Estate: A View from Chatsworth*, Macmillan, London, 1990
Discovering Derbyshire: The Derbyshire Environmental Resources Guide, Derby County Council, Matlock, 1994 (2nd ed.)
Doyle, Arthur Conan, 'The Terror of Blue John Gap', *The Strand Magazine*, August 1910
Drayton, Michael, *Poly-Olbion*, Marriott, Grismand & Dewe, London, 1622
Edwards, K.C., *The Peak District* (New Naturalist Series), Collins, Glasgow, 1962
Ford, Trevor D., and Rieuwerts, J.H., *Lead Mining in the Peak District*, Peak Park Planning Board, Bakewell, 1968
Harris, Helen, *Industrial Archaeology of the Peak District*, Ashbourne Editions, Ashbourne, 1971
Heape, R Grundy, *Buxton Under the Dukes of Devonshire*, Hale, London, 1948
Kirkham, Nellie, *Derbyshire* (Vision of England series), Elek, London, 1947
Leyland, John, *The Peak of Derbyshire*, Seeley, London, 1891
Marsden, Barry M., *The Barrow Knight*, K.M. Publications, 1988
Matlock and the Peak District (Red Guide), Ward Lock, London, 1963
Mee, Arthur, *Derbyshire* (King's England series), Hodder & Stoughton, London, 1937
Mee, Arthur, *Yorkshire: West Riding* (King's England series), Hodder & Stoughton, London, 1941
Merrill, John N., *Customs of the Peak District & Derbyshire*, Trail Crest, Winster, 1993
Merrill, John N., *Derbyshire Folklore*, Footprint Press, Ripley, 1995
Milburn, Geoff, (ed.), *Peak Rock Climbs, Volume 3*: Froggatt, British Mountaineering Council, Manchester, 1991
Morgan, Philip, (ed.), *Domesday Book: Derbyshire*, Phillimore, Chichester, 1978
Morris, Christopher, (ed.), *The Journeys of Celia Fiennes*, Cresset Press, London, 1947
Morris, John, (ed.), *Domesday Book: Staffordshire*, Phillimore, Chichester, 1976

Nelthorpe, T., *The Kinder Log*, Cicerone Press, Milnthorpe, 1987
Pevsner, Nikolaus, (Williamson, Elizabeth, rev.), *Derbyshire* (Buildings of England series), Penguin Books, Harmondsworth, 1978 (1st pub. 1953)
Pevsner, Nikolaus, *Staffordshire* (Buildings of England series), Penguin Books, Harmondsworth, 1974
Pevsner, Nikolaus, (Radcliffe, Enid, rev.) *Yorkshire: The West Riding* (Buildings of England series), Penguin Books, Harmondsworth, 1967 (1st pub. 1959) 1974
Porteous, Crichton, *The Beauty and Mystery of Well-Dressing*, Pilgrim Press, Derby, 1949
Porteous, Crichton, *Peakland*, Robert Hale, London, 1954
Porter, Lindsey, *The Peak District: Its Secrets & Curiosities*, Moorland Publishing, Ashbourne, 1988
Porter, Lindsey, *A Visitor's Guide to the Peak District*, Moorland Publishing, Ashbourne, 1994 (1st pub. 1982)
Poucher, W.A., *The Peak & Pennines*, Constable, London, 1966
Poucher, W.A., *Peak Panorama: Kinder Scout to Dovedale*, Chapman & Hall, London, 1946
Price, Norman, *The Derbyshire Dales*, Warne, London, 1953
Redfern, Roger, *Peak District Hill Country*, Sigma, Wilmslow, 1993
Redfern, Roger, *Peakland Days*, Robert Hale, London, 1970
Redfern, Roger, *A Picture of the Peak District*, Robert Hale, London, 1987
Redhead, Brian, *The Peak: A Park For All Seasons*, Constable, London, 1989
Robinson, Brian, (ed.), *The Seven Blunders of the Peak*, Scarthin Books, Cromford, 1994
Robson, Les, *A Gazetteer of the White Peak*, Hall, Derby, 1991
Scarf, Norman, *Innocent Espionage: The La Rochefoucauld Brothers' Tour of England in 1785*, Boydell Press, Woodbridge, 1995
Sellers, Gladys, *Walking in the South Pennines*, Cicerone, Milnthorpe, 1991
Smith, Roland, *First and Last*, Peak Park Joint Planning Board, Bakewell, 1978
Smith, Roland, *The Peak National Park*, Webb & Bower, Exeter, 1987
Smith, Roland, *Time Exposure: The Peak National Park – Past and Present*, Peak Park Joint Planning Board, Bakewell, 1991
Thompson, Francis, *Chatsworth: A Short History*, Country Life, London, 1951
Thorne, James, *Rambles by Rivers: The Dove*, Knight, London, 1846
Thorold, Henry, *A Shell Guide: Derbyshire*, Faber, London, 1972
Thorold, Henry, *A Shell Guide: Staffordshire*, Faber, London, 1978
Wainwright, A., *Pennine Way Companion*, Westmorland Gazette, Kendal, 1968
Walton, Izaak, & Cotton, Charles, *The Compleat Angler*, O.U.P., Oxford, 1935 (1st pub. 1676)
Wardley, C.F., *The Rambler's Guide to Buxton and Neighbourhood*, 'Advertiser' Offices, Buxton, c.1906

Index